The Art of
String Figures

International String Figure Association

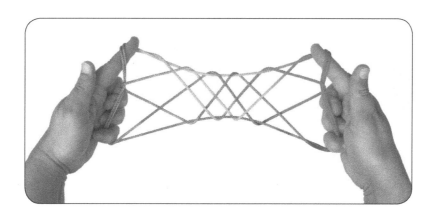

DOVER PUBLICATIONS, INC.
Mineola, New York

Contents

Bibliographical Note

The Art of String Figures, first published by Dover Publications, Inc., in 2018, is an original compilation of material first published in issues of *String Figure Magazine* (ISFA Press, Pasadena, California), in 2006 and 2007.

The International String Figure Association was founded in 1978. For membership information, write to ISFA, P.O. Box 5134, Pasadena, CA 91117 or visit ISFA online at www.isfa.org.

Library of Congress Cataloging-in-Publication Data

Names: International String Figure Association.
Title: The art of string figures / International String Figure Association.
Other titles: String figure magazine.
Description: Mineola, New York : Dover Publications, Inc., 2018. | "The Art of String Figures, first published by Dover Publications, Inc., in 2018, is an original compilation of material first published in issues of String Figure Magazine (ISFA Press, Pasadena, California), in 2006 and 2007."
Identifiers: LCCN 2018017153| ISBN 9780486829166 | ISBN 0486829162
Subjects: LCSH: String figures.
Classification: LCC GV1218.S8 A78 2018 | DDC 793.9/6—dc23
LC record available at https://lccn.loc.gov/2018017153

Manufactured in the United States by LSC Communications
82916203   2019
www.doverpublications.com

Getting Started

Fingers, Loops, Strings, and Commands

String figures are made with an endless loop. The size that is best for you depends on how big you are and the complexity of the design you are making.

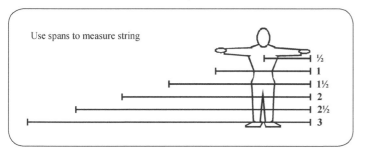

Use spans to measure string

A span is the distance between the tips of your hands when your arms are outstretched, as shown. A loop made from a 1-span string works well for most string figures. Simpler figures require a loop made from a ½-span string. Complicated designs can require loops made from 1½, 2, 2½, or even 3-span strings.

flame

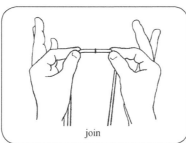

join

To join the ends of a string made from synthetic fibers (eg, nylon, polyester), flame the ends until they melt (with adult supervision), then touch them together. For a string made from natural fibers (eg, cotton, hemp), use molten nylon as glue.

Each step of the weaving process is illustrated. We use *arrows* to show what your fingers and hands should do to advance to the next step.

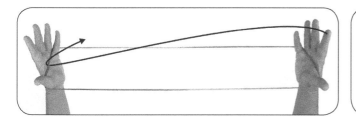

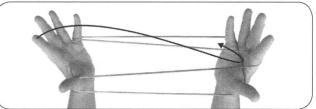

Often you will need to *release* a loop and *extend* the figure (separate your hands to absorb the slack). We use a *black square* ■ to indicate which finger should release its loop.

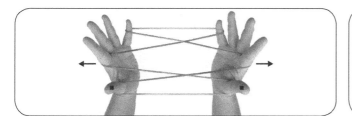

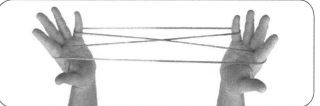

Whenever an arrow and a black square appear in the same illustration, perform the action illustrated by the arrow first. An arrow-square combination often indicates a loop transfer.

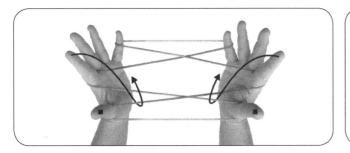 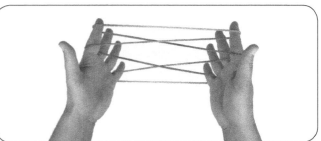

Although you should be able to make all the string figures by looking at the pictures, we've supplied written instructions in case you get stuck. Abbreviations and terms are summarized below.

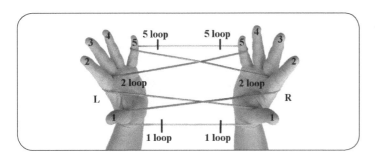

The fingers of each hand are numbered 1 to 5.

L stands for *Left*. R stands for *Right.*

Loops are named after the fingers they surround.

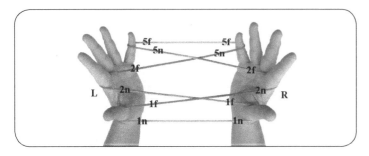

Each loop has a *near* string (n) and a *far* string (f).

The near string is the string closest to finger 1. The far string is the string closest to finger 5.

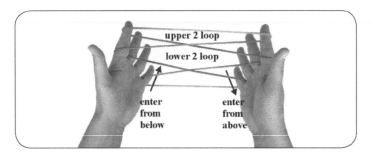

Loops can be entered from *above* (the side nearest the fingertip) or *below* (the side nearest the knuckle).

When two loops surround a finger, the loop nearest the fingertip is the *upper* loop. The loop nearest the knuckle is the *lower* loop.

Perform all actions with both hands simultaneously. If an R or an L precedes a finger, loop, or string name, perform the action on the indicated hand only.

Lightning

collected by Sir Raymond Firth from the people of the Solomon Islands

RECOMMENDED STRING LENGTH: 1½ SPANS

This action figure is known throughout the Pacific. The initial pattern, which represents heavy rain, can be partially dissolved and reformed over and over again.

 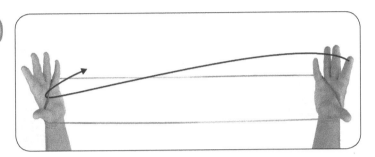

Place loop on 1 and 5 (*Position 1*).

R2 picks up L palmar string.

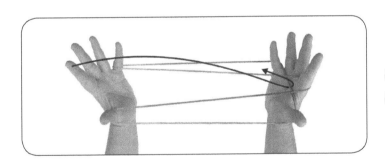

L2, through R2 loop from above, picks up R palmar string.

 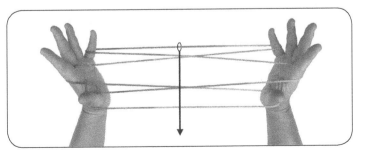

You now have *Opening A*.

Mouth, over all strings, bites center of 5f and returns.

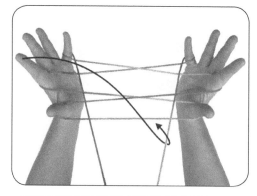

L2, over intervening strings, picks up R mouth string and returns.

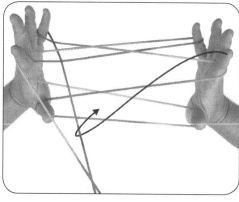

R2, over intervening strings, picks up L mouth string and returns.

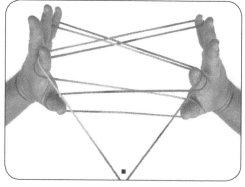

Mouth releases its loop.

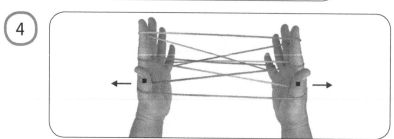

1 releases its loop. Hands separate to absorb the slack.

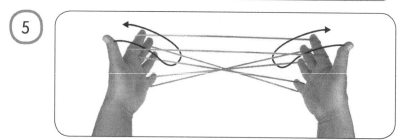

1, through lower 2 loop from above, picks up lower and upper 2f and returns under upper 2n.

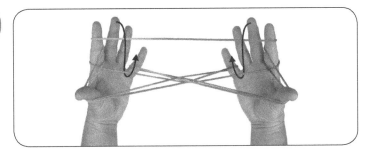

3, over upper 2n, picks up lower 2n.

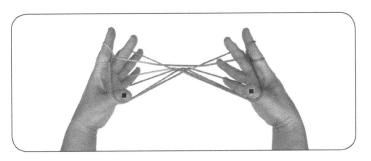

1 gently releases its loops to form hanging strings.

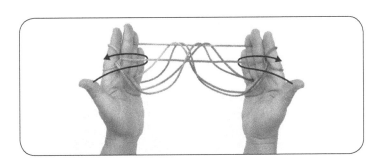

1, over hanging strings, picks up upper 2n.

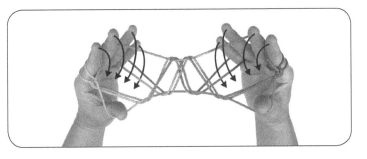

4 and 5 hook down 3f. (5 enters its own loop from above.) 2 and 3 also touch the palm to complete the extension.

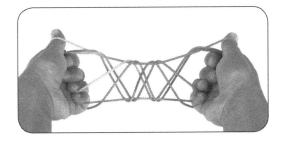

The vertical lines that span the frame strings represent the heavy rain of a thunderstorm.

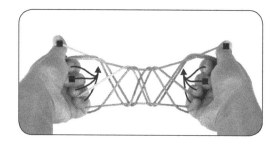

To simulate the sudden appearance of lightning, quickly unfold 2, 4, and 5 while simultaneously releasing the loops from 1 and 3. This definitely requires practice and coordination!

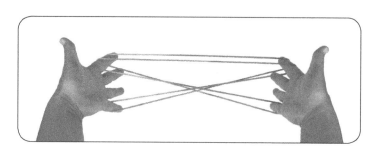

The pattern dissolves.

Repeat steps 5–10 over and over to simulate rain followed by bursts of lightning. (Include appropriate sound effects.)

Net Broken, Net Repaired

collected by Diamond Jenness from the Papuans of Goodenough Island

RECOMMENDED STRING LENGTH: 1½ SPANS

When making a complex string figure, Melanesians often remove loops from each hand and reset them in a different order to achieve a desired arrangement. The following figure is prime example. In this rather long series, an action figure is formed that represents two fish swimming apart. According to legend, the fish escaped from a net that had a hole in it. Next, the figure is partially dissolved and the entire weaving sequence is repeated. Remarkably, a different figure appears. The second figure represents an intact net. (No escaping fish are seen.)

①

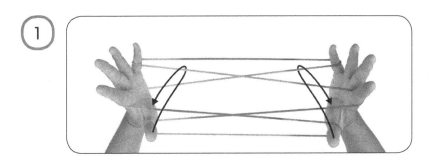

Begin with *Opening A.* (See "Lightning" on page 1.)

1, over 2 loop, picks up 5n.

②

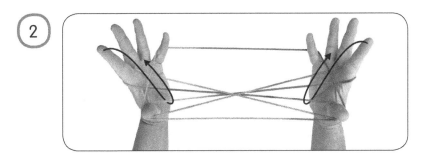

2 picks up lower 1f.

③

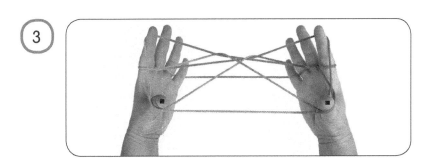

1 releases its loops.

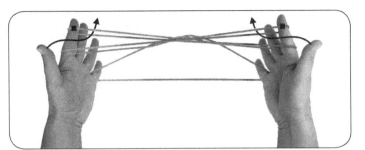

1, from below, removes upper 2 loop.

 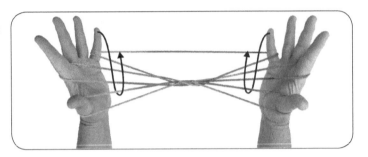

5, over 2 loop, picks up 1f.

 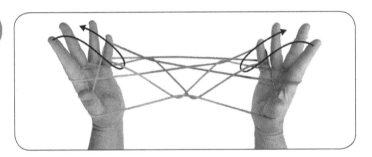

2 picks up lower 5n.

 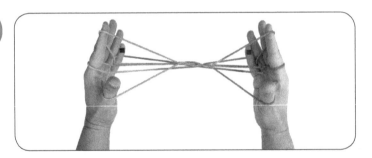

5 releases its loops.

 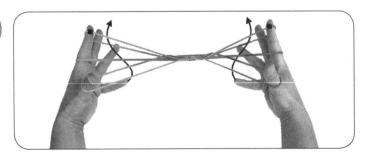

5, from below, removes upper 2 loop.

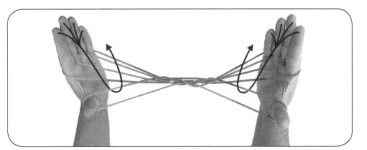

2345, from below, enters the 1 loop. (1 loop becomes a wrist loop.)

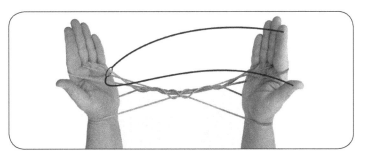

R1 and R2 grasp L2f and L5n.

L hand gently releases all its loops.

L1 enters the former L wrist loop from the opposite side of where the L hand passed through it. L2 and L5 enter their former loops from the same side through which they originally passed.

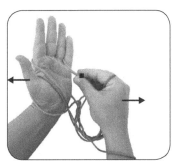

L hand returns to its original position.

R1 and R2 release the strings they are holding. Hands separate to absorb the slack.

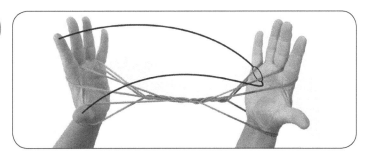

Likewise, L1 and L2 grasp R2f and R5n.

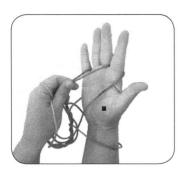 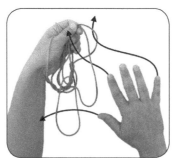

R hand gently releases all its loops.

R1 enters the former R wrist loop from the opposite side of where the R hand passed through it. R2 and R5 enter their former loops from the same side through which they originally passed.

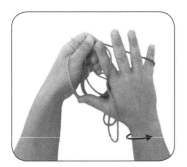 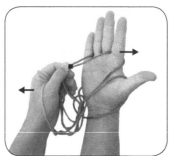

R hand returns to its original position.

L1 and L2 release the strings they are holding. Hands separate to absorb the slack.

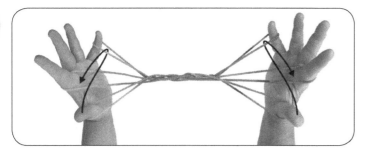

1, over 2 loop, picks up 5n.

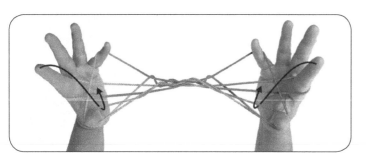

Now do the *Caroline Extension*:

2 picks up lower 1f.

1 presses against the side of 2 to trap the string that runs from 1 to 2 *and* the string that runs from 1 to 5.

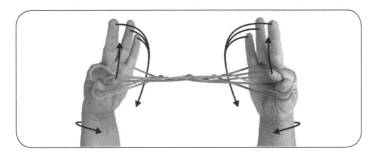

As 2 returns, 345 folds down over 5f and wrists turn so that upper 2f and 5f form frame strings.

You now have four diamonds bisected by a pair of horizontal strings.

The Papuans of Goodenough Island failed to name this pleasing figure, but the design is widely known throughout the Pacific, where it is made by a variety of methods.

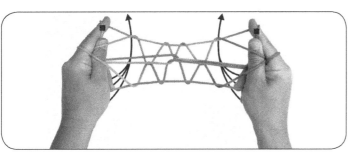

To continue, undo the *Caroline Extension*. (Release the upper 2 loop and unfold 345.)

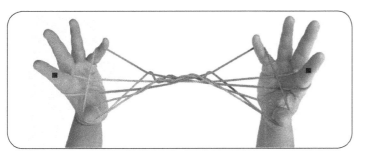

Action: Gently release the 2 loop . . .

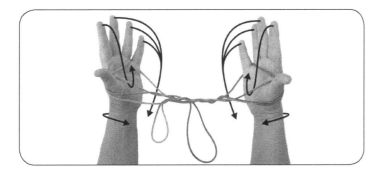

. . . and repeat the *Caroline Extension*.

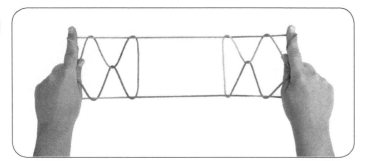

Two "fish" swim apart as the hands are separated.

The maker intended to make a four-diamond figure representing a net. As you can see, the net is bad (it breaks in the middle) and the fish escape.

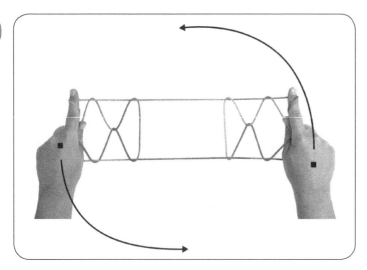

To repair the net, proceed as follows:

Rotate the figure a quarter turn counterclockwise and lay the figure on a flat surface, releasing the hands entirely.

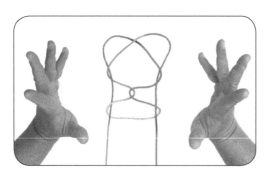

Position the hands so that the former right-hand fish is between them.

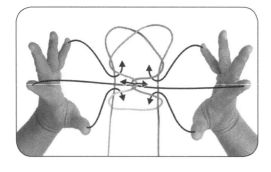

1 and 5, from above, enter the triangle between the fish's body and tail. Then 5 picks up the oblique string that forms the fish's back, while 1 picks up the oblique string that forms the fish's tail. 2, over the frame lines, enters the small space between the interlocking loops found at the junction of the fish's body and tail.

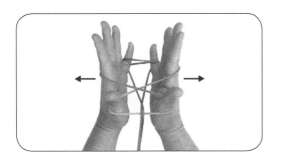

Hands separate, lifting the figure off the flat surface.

You now have a three-loop opening that resembles *Opening A*, but with a subtle difference.

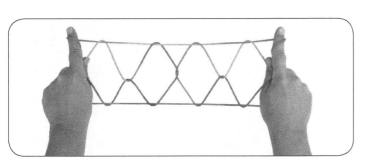

If you repeat the entire weaving sequence (steps 1–18), a four-diamond figure will result. The net is repaired!

Raise the Eyebrows

collected by Sir Raymond Firth from the people of the Solomon Islands

RECOMMENDED STRING LENGTH: 1½ SPANS

In this amusing figure, which represents a person raising his or her eyebrows, the amount of tension applied to the little finger loops is altered. As a result, the strings shift and a second design appears. Loop length plays a critical role here. If the loop is too short or too long, the strings will not shift properly.

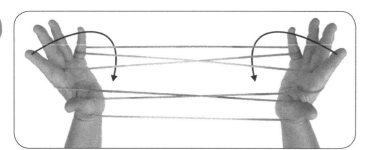

Begin with *Opening A*. (See "Lightning" on page 1.)

2, over 5 loop, catches 5f, 5n, and 2f on its tip and hooks these three strings toward you.

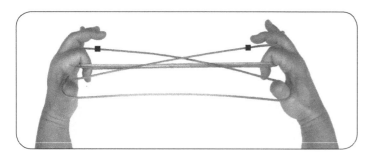

The 2 loop slips over the first joint and onto the tip of 2.

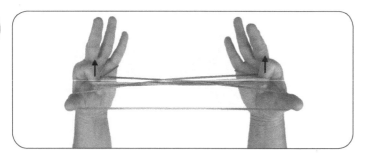

Raise hooked 2 so that its tip is above 1f.

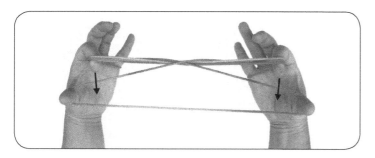

Enter the 1 loop from above. With the tip of 2 catch 1f . . .

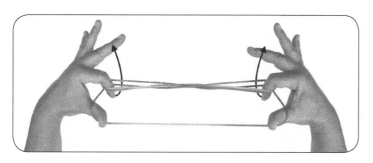

. . . and drag it away from you, rotating 2 away and up.

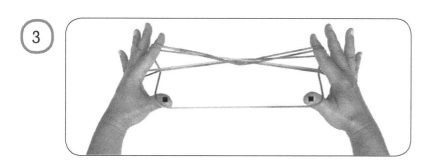

1 releases its loop.

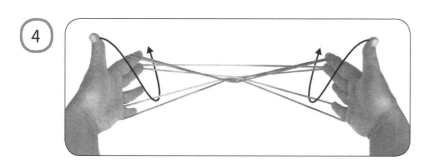

1, under both 2 loops, enters 5 loop from below.

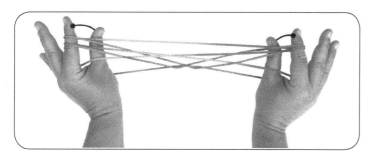

1, on the far side of both 2 loops, presses its tip against the tip of 2.

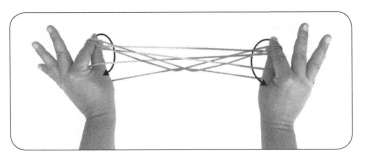

1 and 2 rotate away from you, passing down through the 5 loop.

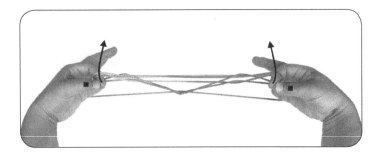

1 and 2 rotate toward you and up. As 2 returns to the upright position, 1 separates from 2.

5

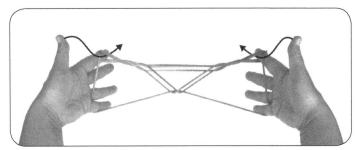

2 now has a double upper loop and a single lower loop that it shares with 5. 1, from below, enters the double upper 2 loop . . .

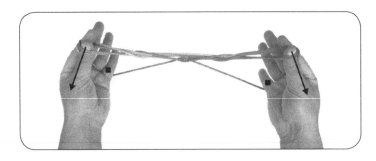

. . . and returns with double upper 2n while 5 releases its loop. Separate 1 from 2 as far as possible to achieve a wide extension.

6

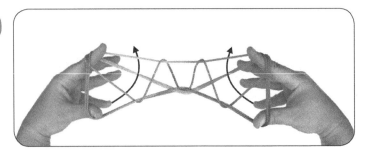

5, from below, enters the 2 loops and returns with double lower 2f strings.

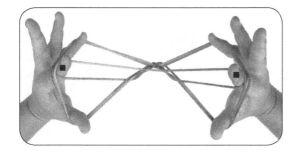

2 releases all of its loops.

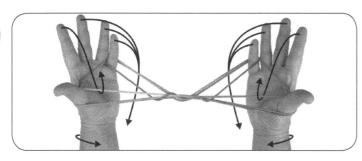

Now do the *Caroline Extension*, as illustrated in "Net Broken, Net Repaired." 2 picks up lower 1f while 1 presses against the side of 2. 345 folds down over 5f, and wrists turn so that 2f and double 5f form frame strings.

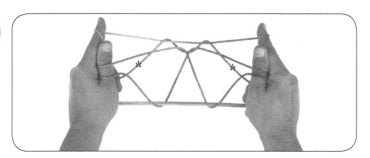

The resulting design represents a squinting face. (Eyes are hidden.)

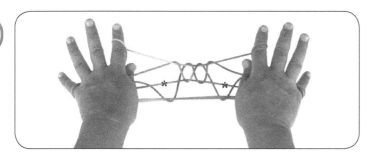

Action: To "raise the eyebrows" and reveal the eyes (a pair of small diamonds), unfold 345 and extend widely with palms facing away. This lengthens the 5 loops.

Upon lengthening the 5 loops, the string labeled with an asterisk in the above photo will curl around the upper frame string and become a transverse horizontal string.

Repeat the *Caroline Extension* as often as desired to make the face squint and unfold.

A Flock of Birds

collected by Sir Raymond Firth from the people of the Solomon Islands

RECOMMENDED STRING LENGTH: 1½ SPANS

In Fiji, this pattern is called "Full Morning" because the design springs into view just like the rising sun. In the Solomon Islands, the figure represents birds that suddenly appear out of nowhere and pause to feed. When startled, the birds scatter in all directions without leaving a trace. The figure dissolves.

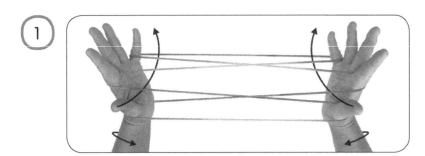

Begin with *Opening A*. (See "Lightning" on page 1.)

1, under 2 loop, enters 5 loop from below.

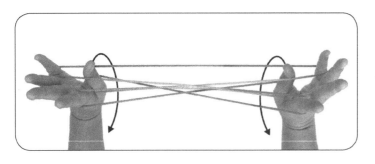

1 passes over 5f and down . . .

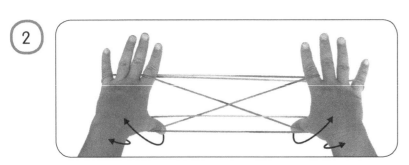

. . . then returns to an upright position, completing a full rotation away from the body. An upper 1 loop is created from 5f in the process.

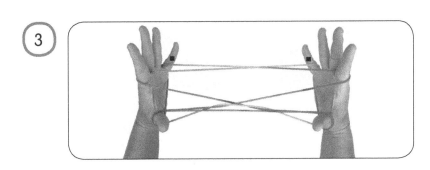

5 releases its loop.

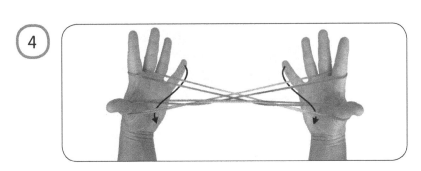

5, under 2 loop, hooks down double 1f.

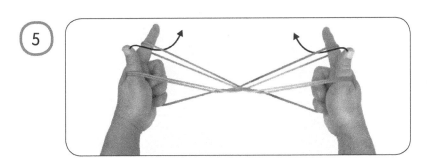

1 picks up 2n.

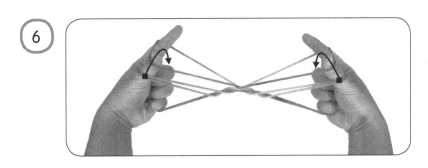

Navajo 1 loops. (Lift the double lower loop over the single upper loop and release it on the far side of 1.)

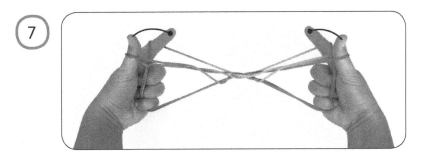

The tip of 1 presses against the tip of 2.

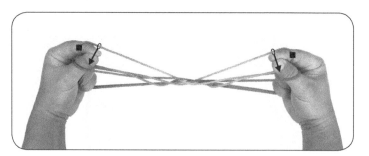

2 transfers its loop to 1.

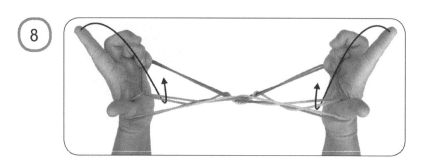

2 picks up oblique strings that resemble double 1f strings.

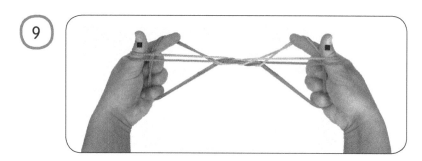

Action: 1 releases its loops sharply while 2 and 5 separate.

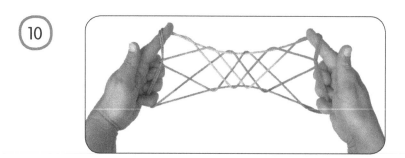

Miraculously, a net-like figure springs into view. Some arranging may be required.

The diamonds represent small birds that spotted food and decided to land suddenly.

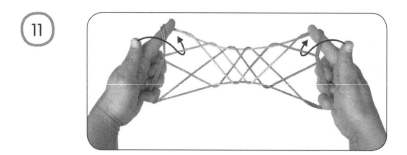

As you know, a flock of birds is easily startled.

Action: 1 picks up the oblique string that runs from the double palmar string to 2f . . .

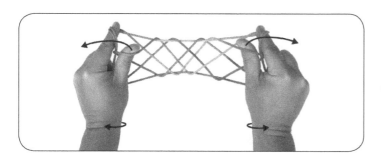

. . . and returns with it.

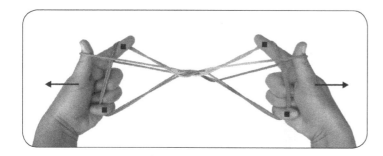

Simultaneously, 2 and 5 release their double loops. Hands separate to absorb the slack.

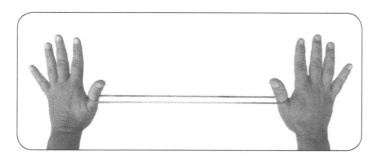

In the blink of an eye the startled birds fly away, leaving nothing more than a simple loop on 1.

Old Man Chewing

collected by Christa de Coppet from the people of the Solomon Islands

RECOMMENDED STRING LENGTH: 1½ SPANS

Simple action figures are often the most effective. In this figure, a triangle represents the mouth of a toothless old man. As thumbs tug on adjacent strings, the triangle contracts and expands, simulating a mouth chewing.

This figure requires a short loop, but most islanders double a longer loop, as we have done here. Throughout the instructions, treat all doubled strings as if they were single.

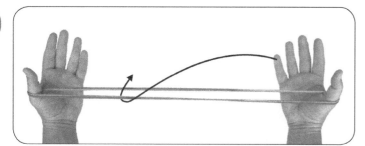

Place a doubled loop on 1.

R5, over L1f and L1n, picks up L1n and returns (but without fully absorbing the slack).

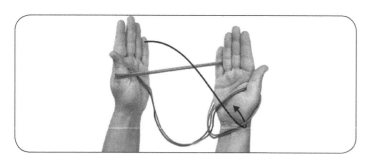

L5, over all intervening strings (including R1n), picks up R1n and returns.

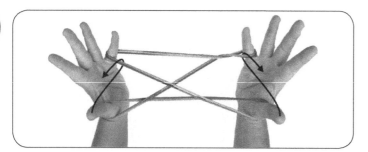

1 picks up 5n.

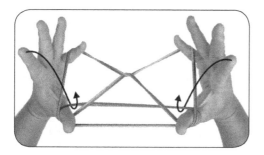

Now do the *Caroline Extension*:

2 picks up lower 1f . . .

. . . then 1 presses against the side of 2 to trap the string that runs from 1 to 2 *and* the string that runs from 1 to 5.

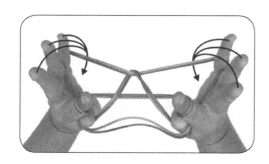

As 2 returns, 345 folds down over 5f.

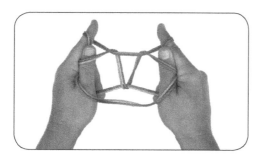

The Solomon Islanders failed to name this pleasing figure, but the design is widely known throughout the Pacific.

To continue, partially undo the *Caroline Extension* by reversing the last two moves. (Unfold 345. Then separate 1 from 2.)

Navajo the 1 loops. (Lift the lower transverse 1n over the upper loop and release it.)

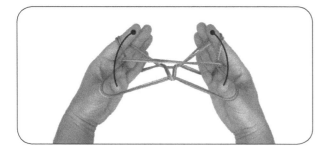

The tip of 1 presses against the tip of 2 . . .

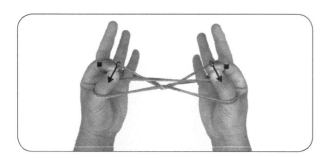

. . . then 2 releases its loop onto 1.

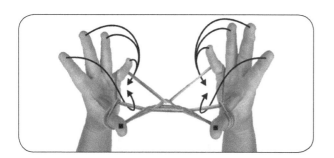

2 picks up the oblique strings that resemble double 1f strings. 1 releases its loops. 345 folds down over 5f.

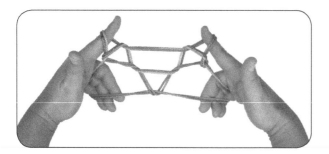

The resulting design represents the face of an old man. The upper triangles are his eyes. The lower triangle is his toothless mouth.

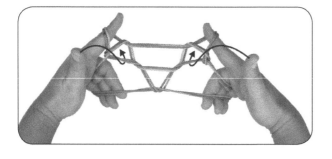

Action: To make the old man chew, 1 picks up the lower string of the nearest "eye" triangle and returns with it. As a result, the "mouth" closes.

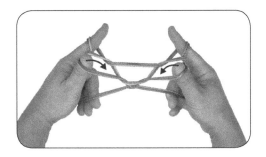

To simulate chewing, 1 repeatedly moves toward the center . . .

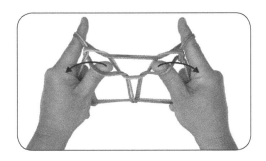

. . . and returns. The mouth repeatedly . . .

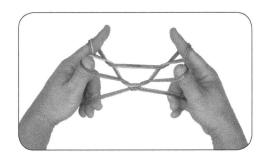

. . . closes . . .

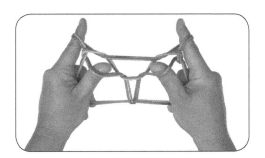

. . . and opens.

Kidnapped Baby

collected by Lyle Dickey from the people of Kauai, Hawaii

RECOMMENDED STRING LENGTH: 1 SPAN

A story accompanies this simple action figure from Kauai in Hawaii. A mother places her baby in a hammock just outside the house so that she can complete her daily chores undisturbed while the baby naps. When the mother returns, she discovers that the baby has been kidnapped. The mourning mother never makes another hammock.

This design belongs to a small family of string figures that requires the maker to rotate one hand a half turn to reveal the final pattern—in this case, a single diamond. That is because, initially, the frames lines are crossed and the pattern is hidden from view. Although awkward to perform, the half rotation successfully uncrosses the frame lines.

On the neighboring island of Niihau, this unique feature gives rise to an amusing alternative name for this figure: "Extreme Shyness." Although the fellow's movements are awkward, the shy one (represented by a diamond) is eventually coaxed into view.

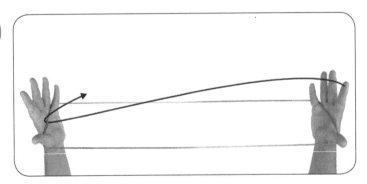

Place loop on 1 and 5 (*Position 1*).

R2 picks up L palmar string.

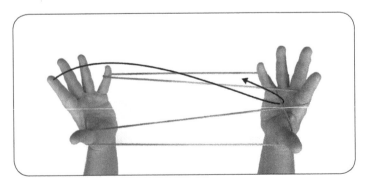

L2, through R2 loop from above, picks up R palmar string.

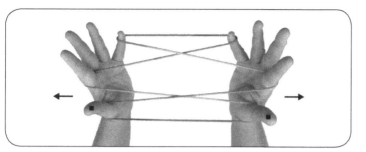

You now have *Opening A*.

1 releases its loop. Hands separate to absorb the slack.

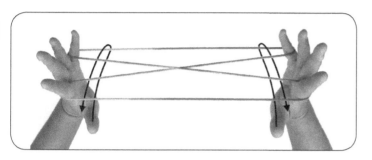

1, under all intervening strings, picks up 5f.

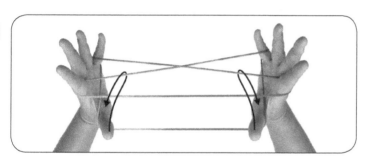

1, over 2n, picks up 2f.

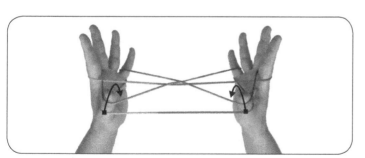

Navajo the loops on 1. (Lift the lower loop over the upper loop and release it on the far side of 1.)

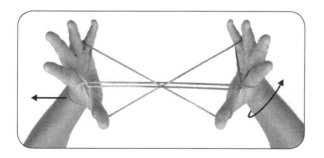

Action: To reveal the baby, rotate the R hand so that the palm faces up and fingers point left. Then shift the entire figure to the left, centering it above the left elbow.

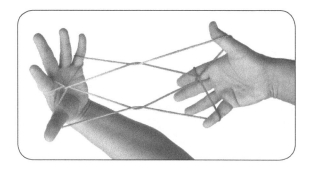

Position the hands as if you were cradling an infant: head held by L hand, spine supported by L arm, and bottom held by R hand. The loops on 1 and 5 represent arms and legs.

Upon revealing the baby, recite the following story:

A mother placed her crying baby in a hammock on the lanai so she could finish her housework. When she returned, the baby was gone and only the hammock remained.

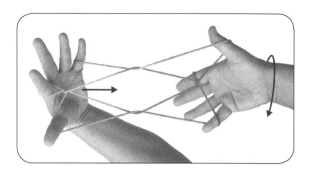

Action: To reveal the empty hammock, return hands to their former position . . .

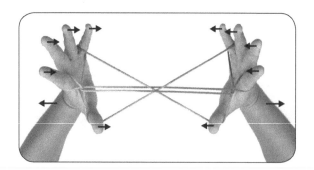

. . . then point the fingertips of each hand toward the opposite hand and spread fingers widely, keeping hands well separated.

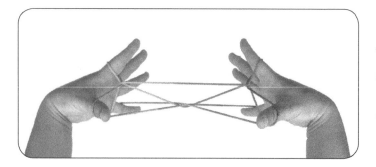

The shallow "V" represents the hammock.

Repeat steps 6 and 7 as often as desired.

Female Turtle, Male Turtle

collected by Willowdean C. Handy from the people of Tahiti, Society Islands

Cyclical string games, in which two or more figures appear over and over in an endless series, are rather uncommon. The Japanese "Cat's Cradle" series is perhaps the most famous example.

"Female Turtle, Male Turtle" is a cyclical action series once known throughout the Society Islands and the adjacent Tuamotus. The series is typically performed by a single player who lays the final patterns on her lap between transformations. However, the series is easily adapted for two players, with one player taking the figure off the hands of a partner as in "Cat's Cradle."

Resist the urge to overextend the female turtle figure: A complex (but beautiful!) knot will result. You can hinder knot formation by securing the frame strings as you separate the hands. (A hint is provided.) With practice, a gorgeous double-walled diamond will appear each time.

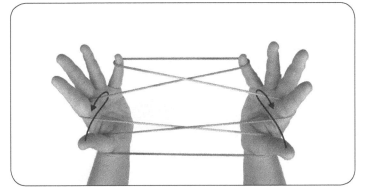

Begin with *Opening A.* (See "Lightning" on page 1.)

1, over 2n, picks up 2f.

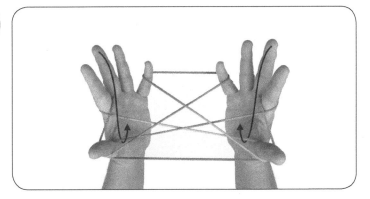

3, over 2n, picks up lower 1f.

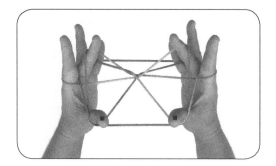

1 releases its loops. Hands separate to absorb the slack.

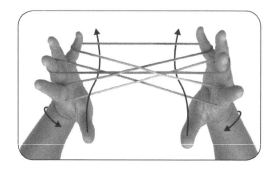

1, through 2 loop from above, passes away from you under all intervening strings . . .

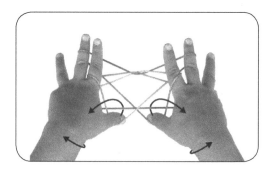

. . . picks up 5f, and returns through the 2 loop.

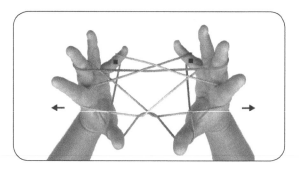

5 releases its loop. Hands separate to absorb the slack.

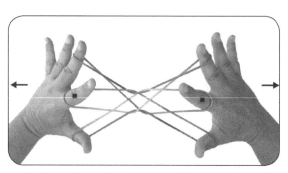

2 releases its loop. Hands separate to absorb the slack.

Hint: To prevent the design from collapsing as it is extended, trap the frame lines by pressing 1 against 2 and 2 against 3 just after releasing the 2 loop.

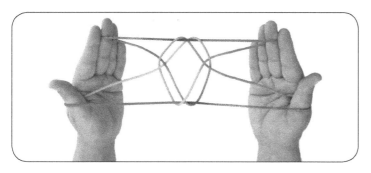

You have a "female turtle." The double-walled diamond represents her petite shell.

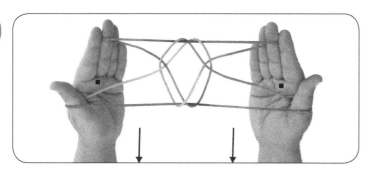

Action: Convert the "female turtle" into a "male turtle" as follows:

With fingers pointing upward, release the figure onto a flat surface.

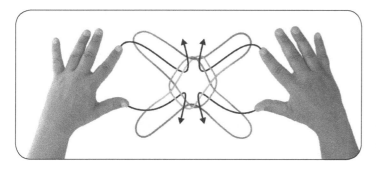

1, from above, enters the single loop nearest you. 2, also from above, enters the single loop farthest from you. 1 and 2, passing under their respective double diamond strings, enter the central diamond from below and return, lifting the figure off the flat surface.

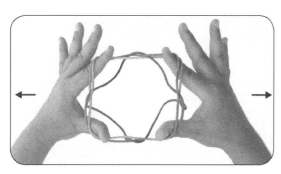

Hands separate to absorb the slack.

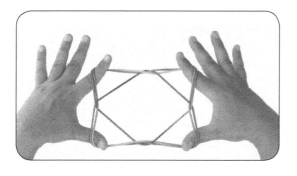

You have a "male turtle." The single-walled diamond represents his shell, which is larger than the female's.

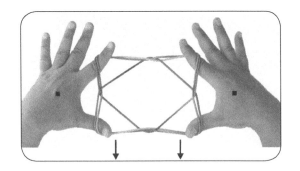

Action: Convert the "male turtle" into a "female turtle" as follows:

With fingers pointing upward, release the figure onto a flat surface.

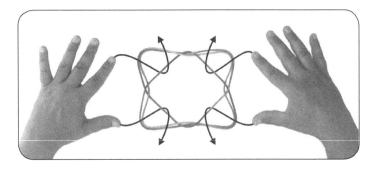

1, from above, enters the double loop nearest you. 2, also from above, enters the double loop farthest from you. 1 and 2, passing under their respective single diamond string, enter the central diamond from below and return, lifting the figure off the flat surface.

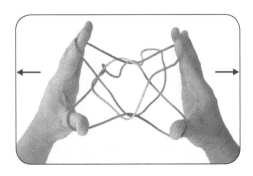

Hands separate to absorb the slack.

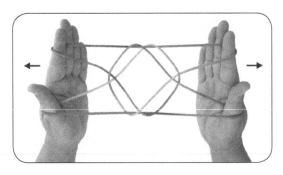

Again you have a "female turtle."

Unlike the male's shell, the female's shell will continue to shrink as you separate the hands.

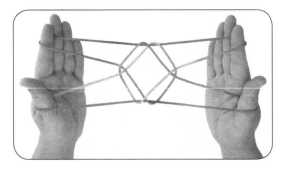

Repeat steps 7 and 8 over and over to alternate between female and male turtles.

Broken Home, Mended Home

collected by Lyle Dickey from the people of Hawaii

RECOMMENDED STRING LENGTH: 1 SPAN

Like many Hawaiian string figures, the story associated with this three-part action series has several layers of meaning. Superficially, the series depicts a house whose roof collapses and is later repaired. On a more profound level, it represents the home of a happy family that is "broken" by a bitter divorce and then reunited once amends have been made. Diamond Jenness collected a similar three-part series from the Inuit of Eastern Siberia, who likewise claimed it represented a house being broken and repaired. The method of construction is entirely different.

①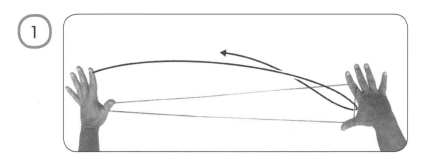

Place loop on L1, R1, and R2.

L2 hooks up the short R1f–R2n string, rotating away and up as it returns to the left.

②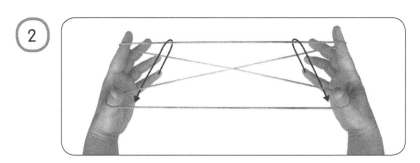

5, under 2f, hooks down 2n, clutching it to the palm.

Resist the urge to use 345 since you will need 3 and 4 later. Keep the 2 loop near the tip of 2.

③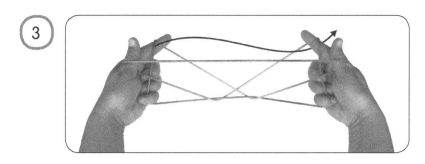

Bringing the tips of 2 together, exchange their loops as follows:

L2, from above, enters the R2 loop and passes to the far side of R2.

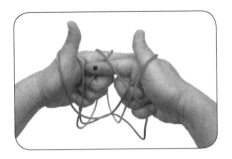

R2 withdraws from its loop, creating a new *lower* loop on L2.

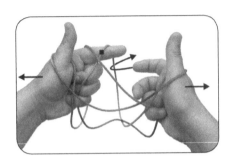

Then R2, from above, removes the upper (original) L2 loop. Hands separate to complete the exchange.

(4)

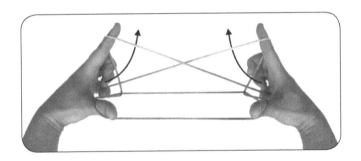

4, passing in front of 2f, enters the 2 loop from below . . .

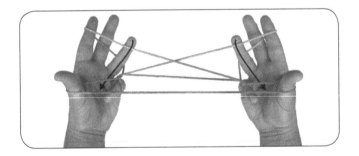

. . . then 4 hooks down 2n, clutching it to the palm.

(5)

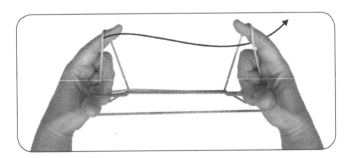

Step 5 is the same as step 3. Bringing the tips of 2 together, exchange their loops as follows:

L2, from above, enters the R2 loop and passes to the far side of R2.

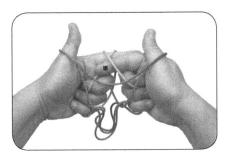

R2 withdraws from its loop, creating a new *lower* loop on L2.

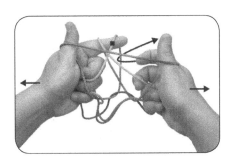

Then R2, from above, removes the upper (original) L2 loop. Hands separate to complete the exchange.

6

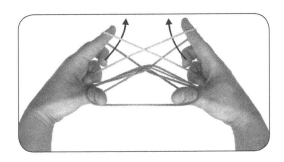

3, passing between 4n and 2f, enters the 2 loop from below.

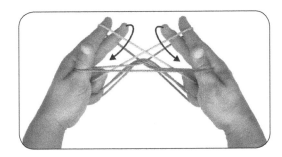

3 hooks down 2n, clutching it to the palm.

7

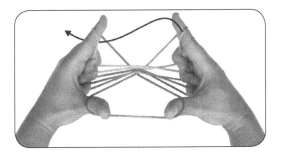

Step 7 is the reverse of step 3. Bringing the tips of 2 together, exchange their loops as follows:

R2, from above, enters the L2 loop and passes to the far side of L2.

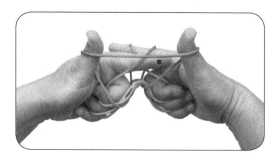

L2 withdraws from its loop, creating a new *lower* loop on R2.

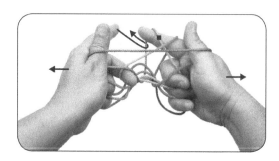

Then L2, from above, removes the upper (original) R2 loop. Hands separate to complete the exchange.

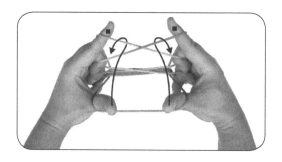

1, from below, removes 2 loop.

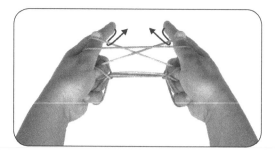

Draw the lower 1 loop through the upper 1 loop as follows:

2 picks up upper 1n to create a temporary 2 loop . . .

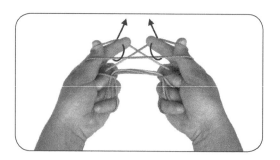

. . . then 2 hooks up lower 1n (a transverse string) and draws it through the temporary 2 loop, which slips off as 2 rotates away and up.

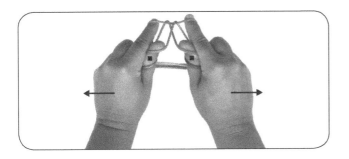

1 releases both of its loops. Hands separate to absorb the slack and reveal the first of three designs.

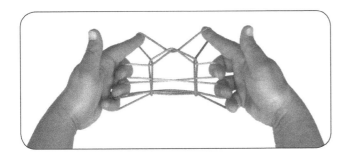

You have "House of a Happy Family." Note that the roof is intact.

10

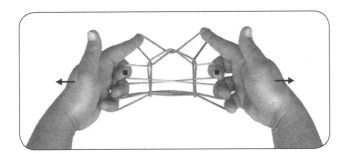

Action: 3 releases its loop. Hands separate to absorb the slack.

11

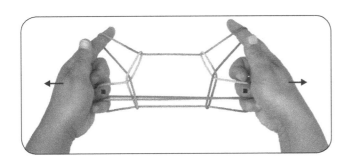

You have "House of a Broken Family." The bent shapes to the right and left represent the separated husband and wife. The roof is no longer intact.

Action: 4 releases its loop. Hands separate to absorb the slack.

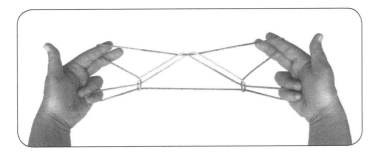

You have "House of a Reunited Family." The husband and wife are no longer separated, and the roof has been mended to make it broader and stronger.

Shark

collected by Kenneth Emory from the people of the Tuamotus

RECOMMENDED STRING LENGTH: 1 SPAN

Throughout the Pacific, sliding string figures often represent fish and other sea creatures. This simple figure from the Tuamotus represents a pesky shark.

The Tuamotu archipelago contains seventy-eight coral atolls, each resembling a shallow turquoise swimming pool in the middle of a deep ocean. In one or two places along the edge of the reef, a deep pass will have opened to allow the tidal currents to enter and leave the central lagoon. These passes also provide entry points for sharks, who love to feed in the calm waters of the lagoon. With only sixteen-thousand permanent inhabitants in the Tuamotus, there are probably more sharks than people!

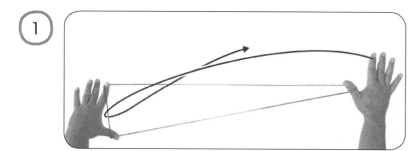

1

Place a loop on R1, L1, and L2.

R2 hooks up the short L1f–L2n string, rotating away and up as it returns to the right.

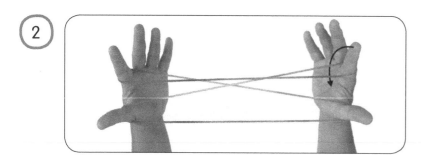

2

Perform the next series of movements as one smooth sequence:

R2 rotates a half turn away so that its tip points downward.

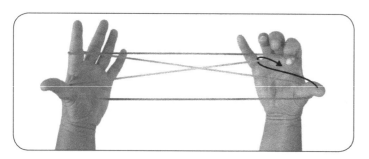

From the fingertip side, R1 enters the inverted R2 loop and returns with R2n.

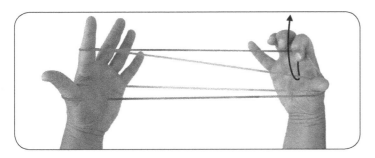

R2 picks up R1f and returns, releasing its inverted loop in the process.

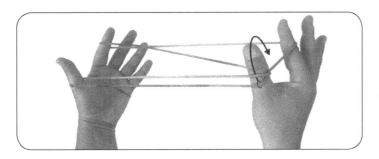

In the final move of this sequence, R1 releases the loop it shares with R2 but retains its single (upper) loop. The easiest way to do this is illustrated below:

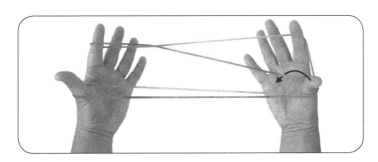

To release the shared R1–R2 loop from R1, bend R1 away over oblique R1f. The shared loop will slip off.

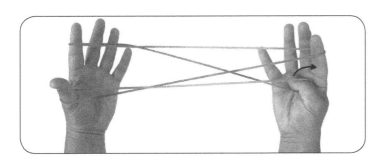

Return R1 to its original position, passing under the newly created R2n string.

(3)

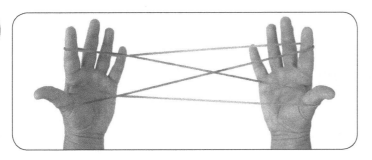

You now have single loops on R1 and R2.

Next, repeat step 2.

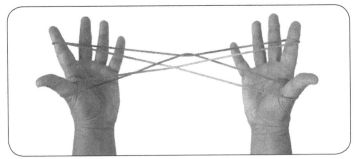

This photo shows the result of repeating step 2.

Now repeat step 2 once more.

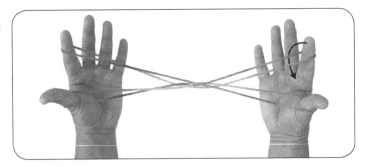

This photo shows the result of performing step 2 a total of three times.

To continue, R2 rotates a half turn away so that its tip points downward.

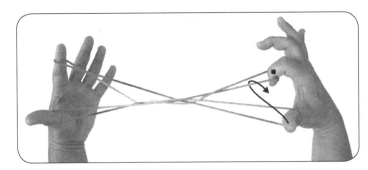

From the fingertip side, R1 removes the inverted R2 loop.

R2345 hooks down double R1f, pressing it firmly against the R palm.

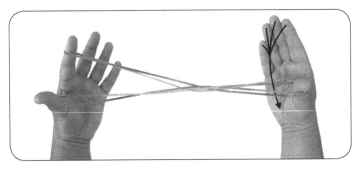

R1 withdraws from the shared double loop.

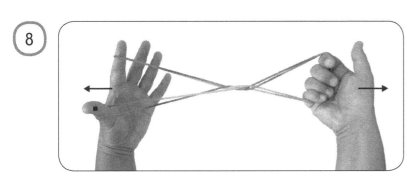

(8) L1 releases its loop. Hands separate to partially absorb the slack.

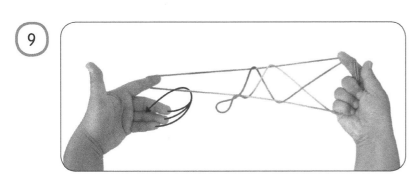

(9) L345 hooks down L2f, pressing it firmly against the L palm.

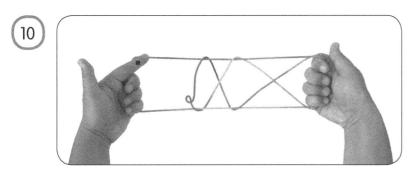

(10) L2 withdraws from the shared loop . . .

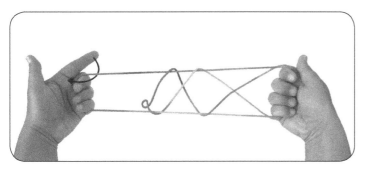

. . . and reenters from the opposite side.

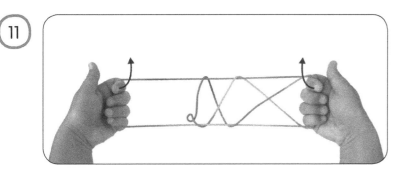

(11) 2 unfolds and presses against the upper frame line to remove all slack from the design.

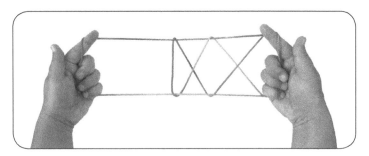

You have a "Shark." The right triangle represents his head. The left triangle represents his tail. The central diamond represents his body and dorsal fin.

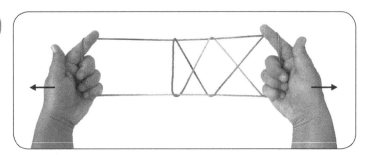

12

Action: The massive shark swims smoothly and steadily through the lagoon. To make the shark swim, separate the hands slowly . . .

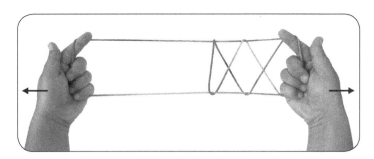

. . . allowing the R hand strings to slide through the R fist.

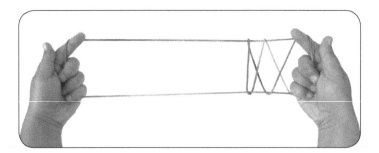

Eventually the shark swims out of sight.

Jumping

collected by Harry and Honor Maude from the people of Kiribati

---

RECOMMENDED STRING LENGTH: 1½ SPANS

Like most string figures, the cord used to make this amusing action figure does not stretch. Nevertheless, the final design behaves like a slingshot! Subtle tension and a precisely timed release cause a loop to jump from the right side of the figure and land on the left thumb.

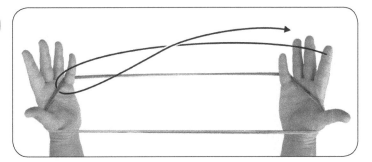

Place a doubled loop on 1 and 5 (*Position I*).

R2 hooks up L palmar string, rotating toward you and up as it returns.

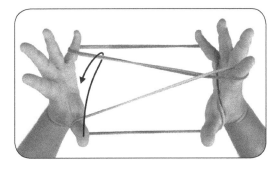

Throughout the following description, treat all doubled strings as if they were single strings.

L1 picks up L5n.

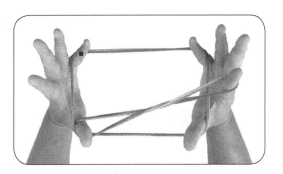

L5 releases its loop.

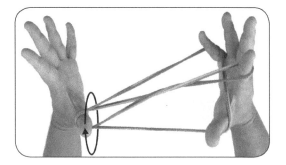

L1 rotates a full turn away from you to introduce a new twist into its loops.

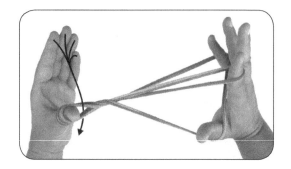

L2345, from above, enters L1 loops and hooks down L1f strings.

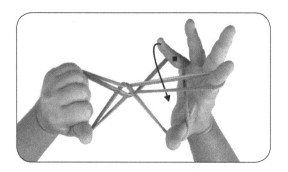

R5, from above, enters the R2 loop and hooks down R2f. In the process, R5 releases its loop.

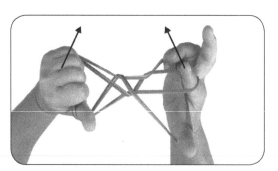

Point forearms away from you . . .

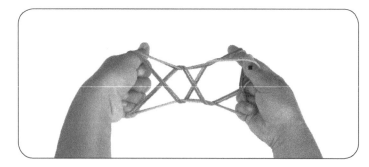

. . . then release the R1 loop to reveal a two-diamond pattern.

8

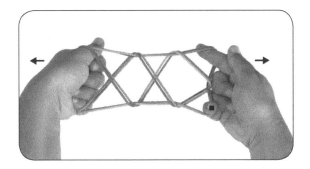

Action: With the figure held taut and R2 held rigid, R5 suddenly releases its loop.

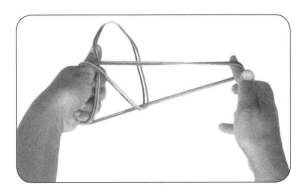

With practice, the two-diamond loop will jump to the left . . .

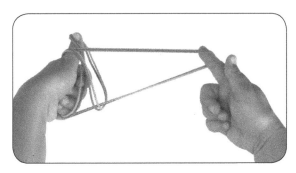

. . . and land on L1.

In Kiribati, the performer shouts, *E tepe!* (It jumps!) The native name for this figure is *Kan Tebe* (about to jump away).

Setting Sun

collected by George A. V. Stanley from the North Queensland Aborigines (Australia)

RECOMMENDED STRING LENGTH: 1½ SPANS

This splendid figure from North Queensland, Australia, represents a ray-adorned sun hovering above the western horizon. In the final action, the sun's light fades to darkness. Once you have mastered the figure, try making it with an even longer string. The "sun" you get may differ depending on the degree of tension you apply during the extension.

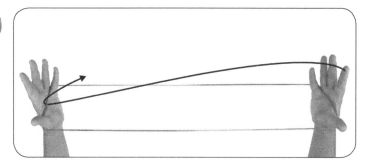

Place loop on 1 and 5 (*Position I*).

R2 picks up L palmar string.

L2, through R2 loop from above, picks up R palmar string.

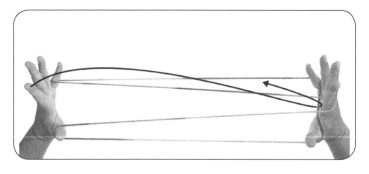

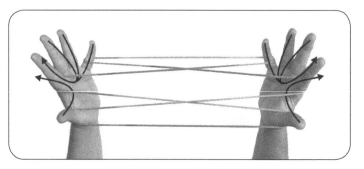

You now have *Opening A*.

1 and 345, from below, enter the 2 loop and allow it to slip down over the 1 loop and 5 loop to become a wrist loop.

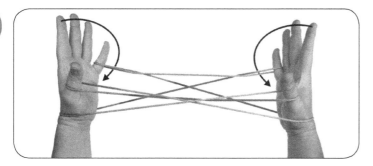

2, passing to the far side of the 5 loop, catches 5f and 5n on its tip and draws these two strings toward you.

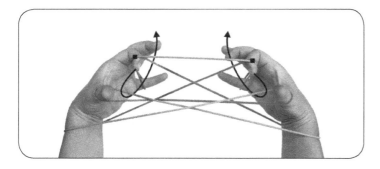

2, still carrying 5f and 5n, enters the 1 loop from above. 2 hooks up 1f by rotating away and up. In the process, 5f and 5n are released from 2.

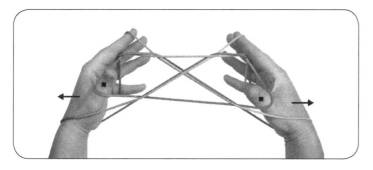

1 releases its loop. Hands separate to absorb the slack.

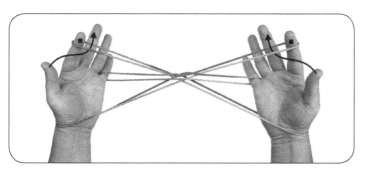

1, from below, removes 2 loop.

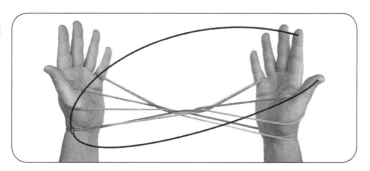

Transfer the L wrist loop to L2 as follows:

R1 and R2 grasp the near string of the L wrist loop . . .

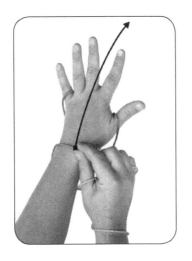

. . . and lift the L wrist loop entirely off the L hand.

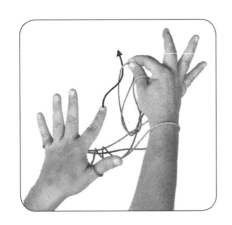

R hand resets the loop it is holding on L2.

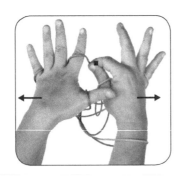

R1 and R2 release the string they are holding. Hands separate to absorb the slack.

6

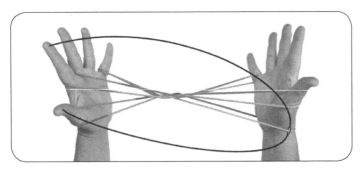

Likewise transfer the R wrist loop to R2 as follows:

L1 and L2 grasp the near string of the R wrist loop . . .

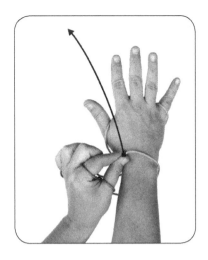

. . . and lift the R wrist loop entirely off the R hand.

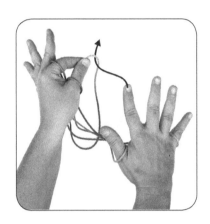

L hand resets the loop it is holding on R2.

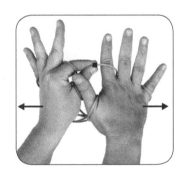

L1 and L2 release the string they are holding. Hands separate to absorb the slack.

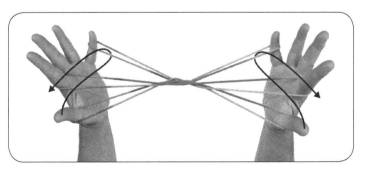

1, over 2 loop, picks up 5n and returns.

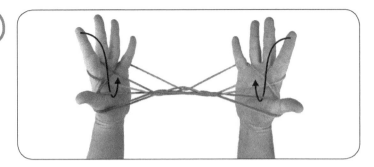

Now do the *Caroline Extension*:

2 picks up lower 1f.

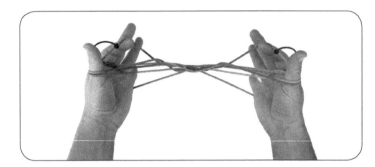

1 presses against the side of 2 to trap the string that runs from 1 to 2 and the string that runs from 1 to 5.

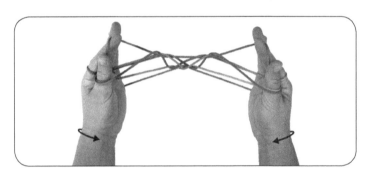

Wrists turn toward the center until palms face away.

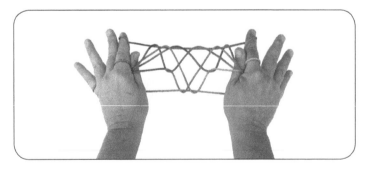

You have "Setting Sun with Rays." The central diamond represents the sun hovering above the western horizon (the lower frame string). The strings emanating from the sun represent rays.

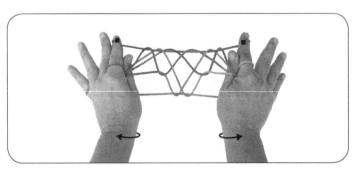

Action: To make the sun set, do the following:

Undo the *Caroline Extension*. Release upper loop from 2 and return hands to the normal position.

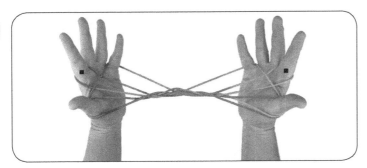

2 gently releases its remaining loop, allowing it to hang freely. (Do not pull taut.)

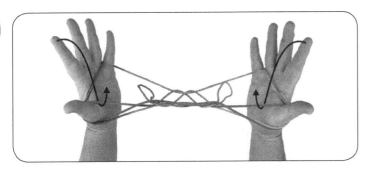

Again do the *Caroline Extension*:

2 picks up lower 1f.

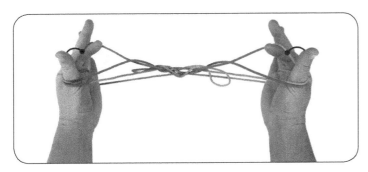

1 presses against the side of 2 to trap the strings located between them.

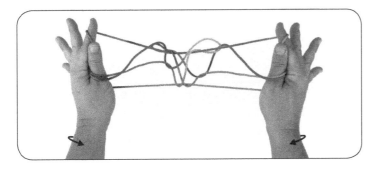

Wrists turn toward the center . . .

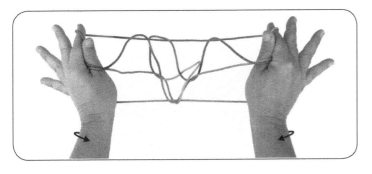

. . . until palms face away and the frame strings are straight.

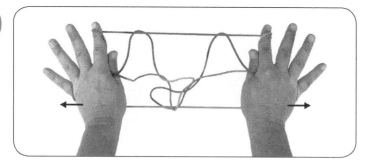

Hands separate slowly to undo the central tangle . . .

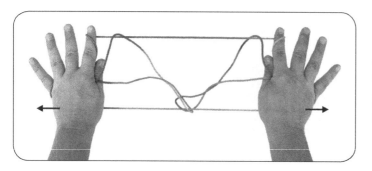

. . . which represents the fading light of the setting sun. Be sure to loosen your grip slightly so that the string can slide through your fingers.

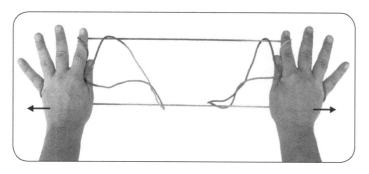

As dusk proceeds, the light (central tangle) continues to break up . . .

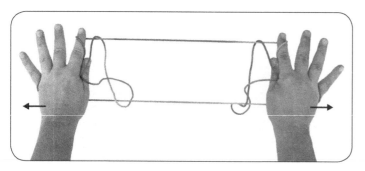

. . . to reveal an empty rectangle . . .

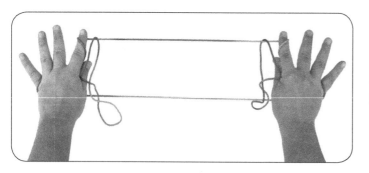

. . . which represents a "Dark Sky after Sunset."

Spindle

collected by Frederick D. McCarthy from the Aborigines of Yirrkala, Arnhem Land (Australia)

RECOMMENDED STRING LENGTH: 1½ SPANS

Drop spindles are primitive spinning tools that were used almost exclusively until about 1000 CE. The spinning wheel did not become popular until the 1500s.

To make this realistic action figure, you will need a loop that has been doubled. (First make a figure eight with a single loop. Then fold it in half.) Throughout the description, treat all doubled strings as if they are single strings. The method collected by McCarthy has been modified somewhat to create a better action figure.

(1)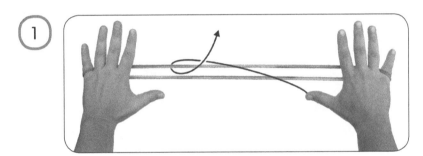

Place a doubled loop on 5 and turn palms away.

R1 passes over L5n and catches this string on its back by rotating toward you and up.

(2)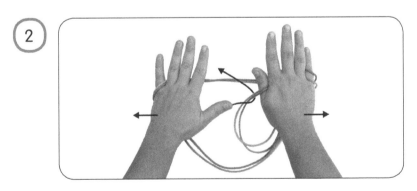

L1, from below, enters the R1 loop and returns with R1n. Hands separate to absorb the slack.

(3)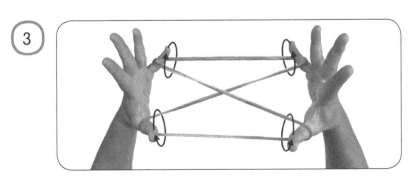

1 rotates a full turn away from you to introduce a twist into its loop.

Likewise, 5 rotates a full turn away from you to introduce a twist into its loop.

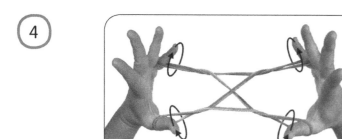

Again, 1 rotates a full turn away from you. This introduces a second twist into its loop.

5 does the same, introducing a second twist into its loop.

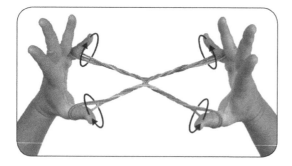

1 and 5 continue to rotate in this fashion to introduce a third . . .

. . . fourth . . .

. . . fifth . . .

. . . and sixth twist into their respective loops.

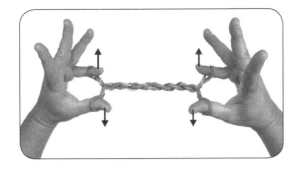

When the loops are as tight as you can get them, the figure is complete.

Action: To see the "Spindle" in motion, separate 1 from 5 as far as possible . . .

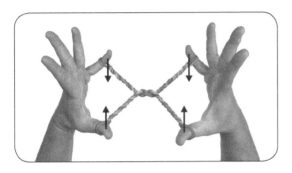

. . . and then bring them together again.

With each repetition . . .

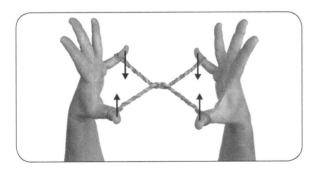

. . . the central strands . . .

. . . coil around the shaft of an imaginary drop spindle.

Leopard's Mouth

collected by Ethel Smith from the people of the Congo

RECOMMENDED STRING LENGTH: 1½ SPANS

In order to display most string figures effectively, the upper and lower frame lines must be separated as far as possible. Pacific Islanders invented the *Caroline Extension* as a means of doing this, but Africans favored the *Mija Extension*, in which loops on index and middle fingers are manipulated.

"Leopard's Mouth" is displayed using a variation of the *Mija Extension*. Instead of loops on the index and middle fingers, loops on the index finger and the wrist are manipulated. The resulting figure is a big, bold, central diamond that contracts and expands with each waggle of the hands.

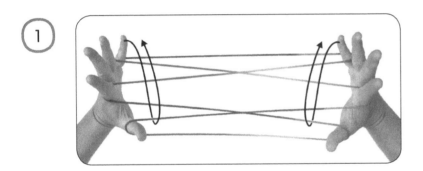

Begin with *Opening A*. (See "Lightning" on page 1.)

5, over 2 loop, picks up 1f.

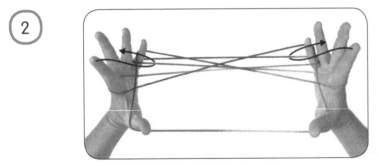

2, over palmar string, picks up lower 5n.

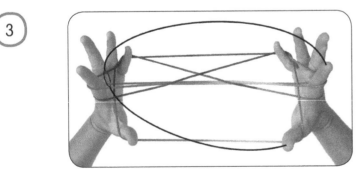

R1 and R2 grasp upper and lower L2f near the base of L2 . . .

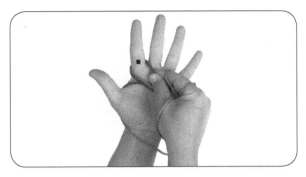

. . . and remove both loops from L2.

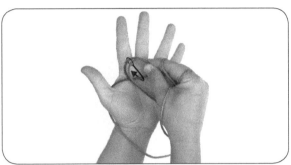

R1 and R2 fold the removed double loop down over the L palmar string, passing their tips between the former lower L2n and L2f strings. Then R1 and R2 pass the double loop they are holding up under the L palmar string . . .

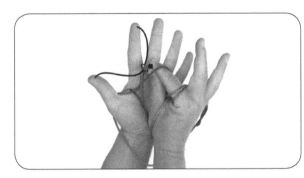

. . . and temporarily give the double loop to L1 and L2.

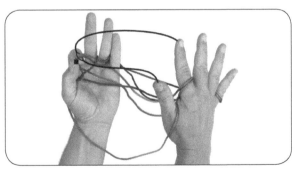

R1 and R2, passing over the L palmar string, recapture the double loop that was temporarily given to L1 and L2.

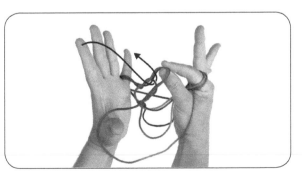

L2 picks up the single string that crosses the base of the double loop held by R1 and R2.

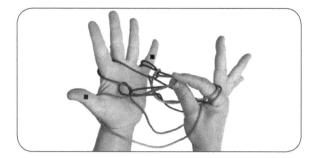

L1 and L5 release their loops.

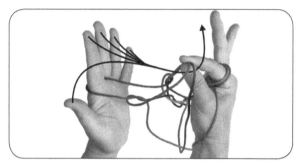

7

L hand, passing from left to right, enters the double loop held by R1 and R2.

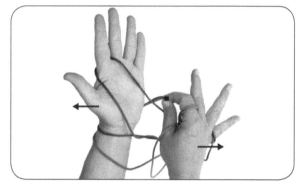

R1 and R2 release the double loop they are holding to create a double L wrist loop. Hands separate to absorb the slack.

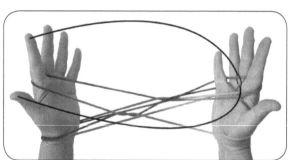

8

Repeat steps 3–7 using opposite hands, as described below:

L1 and L2 grasp upper and lower R2f near the base of R2 . . .

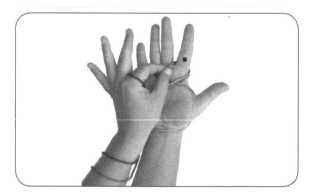

. . . and remove both loops from R2.

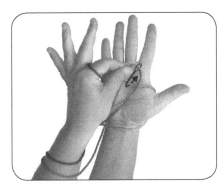

L1 and L2 fold the removed double loop down over the R palmar string, passing their tips between the former lower R2n and R2f strings. Then L1 and L2 pass the double loop they are holding up under the R palmar string . . .

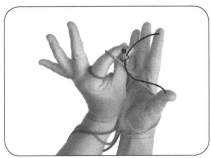

. . . and temporarily give the double loop to R1 and R2.

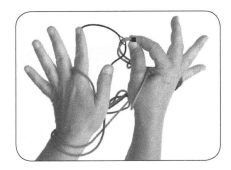

L1 and L2, passing over the R palmar string, recapture the double loop that was temporarily given to R1 and R2.

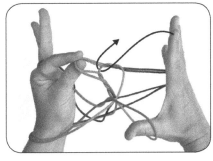

R2 picks up the single string that crosses the base of the double loop held by L1 and L2.

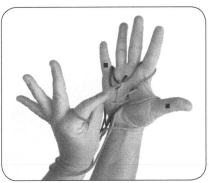

R1 and R5 release their loops.

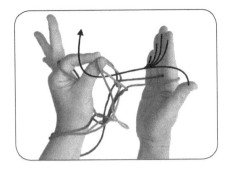

R hand, passing from right to left, enters the double loop held by L1 and L2.

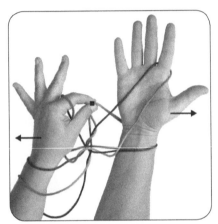

L1 and L2 release the double loop they are holding to create a double R wrist loop. Hands separate to absorb the slack.

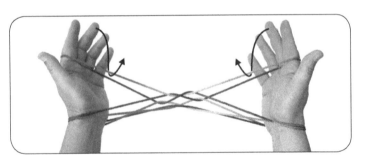

3, over 2f, picks up 2n.

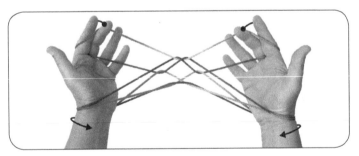

2 presses against the side of 3 to secure the string they share. Then hands rotate so that palms point slightly away.

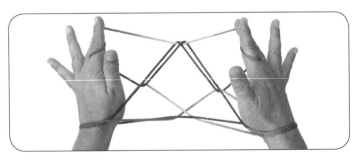

You have "Leopard's Mouth." The central diamond represents his ferocious wide-open mouth.

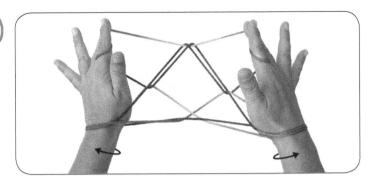

Action: To make the leopard roar, repeatedly rotate your wrists so that . . .

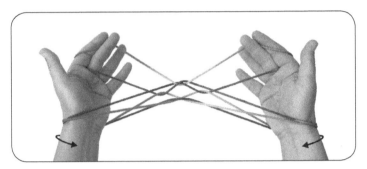

. . . palms alternately face toward you . . .

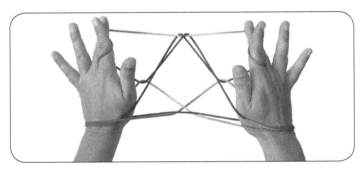

. . . and away. The central diamond contracts and expands, imitating the mouth of a roaring leopard.

Rubber Band

collected by Will Wirt from the people of Lhasa, Tibet

RECOMMENDED STRING LENGTH: 1 SPAN

This amusing action figure is widely known in Tibet, China, and Japan. It consistently represents something made of rubber, elastic, or a sticky substance like gum. The string itself does not stretch, but it appears to do so as the final design is worked by repeatedly bunching and stretching the fingers. It's an optical illusion that amazes many onlookers.

The figure is often preceded by one or more intermediate stages, some of which are named. The initial weaving process has a rhythm that is easy to remember and somewhat reminiscent of "Jacob's Ladder."

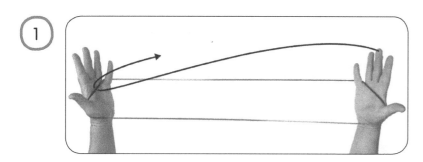

Place loop on 1 and 5 (*Position 1*).

R3 picks up L palmar string.

L3, through R3 loop from above, picks up R palmar string.

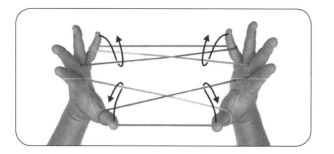

You now have *Japanese Opening A*.

1 picks up 3n. 5 picks up 3f.

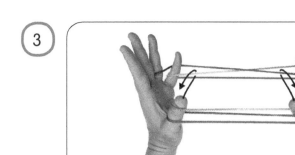

1 picks up lower 5n.

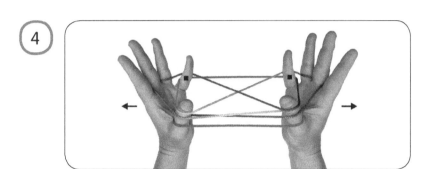

5 releases its loops. Hands separate slightly to absorb the slack.

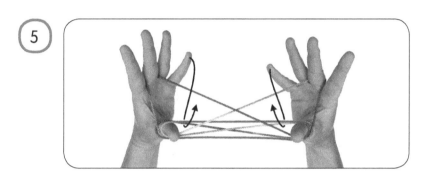

5, over 3f, picks up both 1f strings.

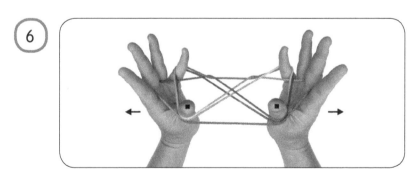

1 releases it loops. Hands separate slightly to absorb the slack.

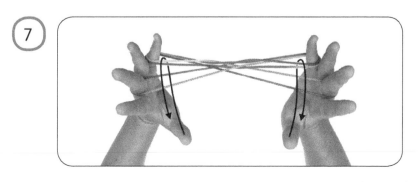

1, over 3 loop, picks up both 5n strings.

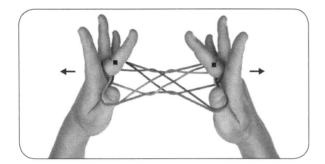

In China, this stage is called "Bridge."

To form the next stage, 3 releases its loop. (Use opposite hands for assistance.) Hands separate to extend the figure.

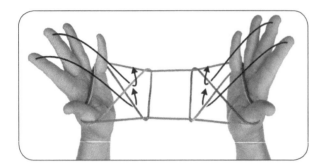

On each side, two strings cross to form an "X." The center is bounded by sliding triangles.

2 and 3, from above, pinch the center of the "X." Then they pass their tips up through the adjacent triangle.

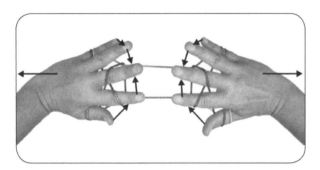

Fingers of each hand bunch together while hands separate to extend the figure.

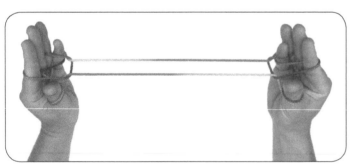

You have "Rubber Band."

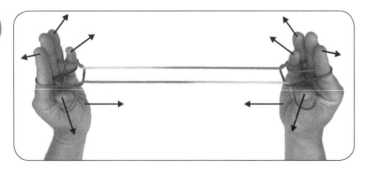

Action: To work the figure, fingers of each hand separate while hands approach each other.

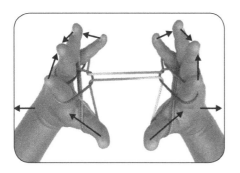

Fingers of each hand bunch together while hands separate.

The two horizontal strings appear to shorten and lengthen as if made of rubber.

13

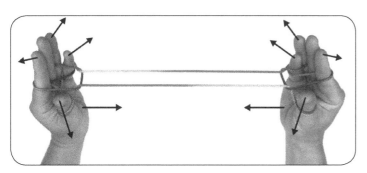

Continue separating . . .

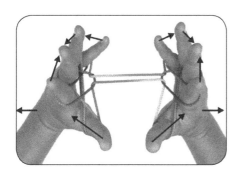

. . . and bunching the fingers to simulate the stretching of a rubber band.

Date

collected by Will Wirt from the people of Dali, China

RECOMMENDED STRING LENGTH: 1 SPAN

This simple action figure is a variation of "Mosquito"—a disappearing knot figure known worldwide. In China the central knot represents a date, the edible fruit of a palm tree.

Before the figure is woven, a "cow hitch" is formed around each middle finger. A cow hitch consists of two opposing half-hitches tied in opposite directions. Once the "Date" is formed, the central knot is dissolved by clapping the hands (which is purely theatrical) and releasing the upper middle finger loops. The date dissolves as the hands separate. This represents eating the date. The action can be repeated over and over once the cow hitches are formed.

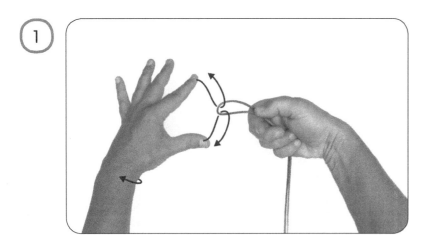

Grasp both strands of the string loop between R1 and R2, about 3 inches from one end, to form a short loop that points toward the left.

Insert L1 and L2, from below, into the short loop, rotating the L wrist so that the L palm faces toward you.

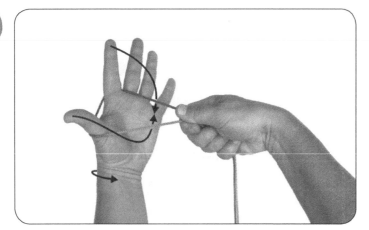

L wrist rotates so that L palm faces away from you. L1 and L2 touch their tips together so that they surround the L1n and L2f strings.

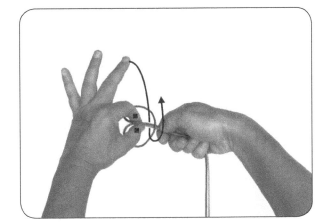

L3, from below (from the knuckle side), removes the L2 loop. L3, from above (from the fingertip side), removes the L1 loop.

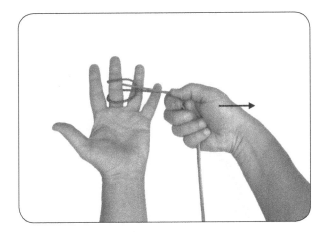

R hand moves right to tighten the cow hitch surrounding L3.

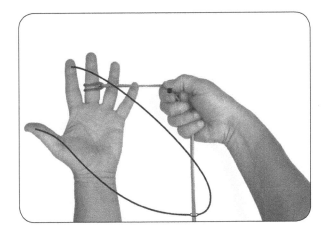

R hand releases its strings. L hand grasps both strands of the hanging loop about 3 inches from its end.

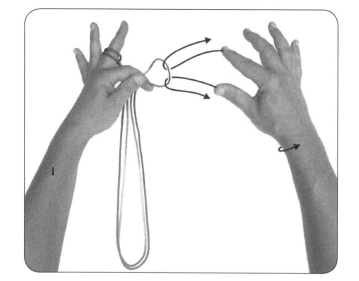

Insert R1 and R2, from below, into the short loop, rotating the R wrist so that the R palm faces toward you.

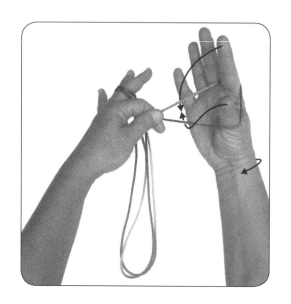

R wrist rotates so that R palm faces away from you. R1 and R2 touch their tips together so that they surround the R1n and R2f strings.

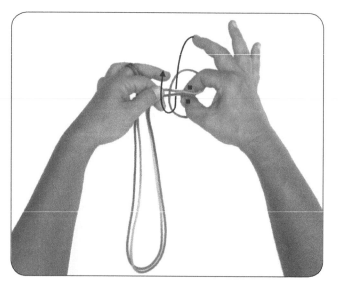

R3, from below (from the knuckle side), removes the R2 loop. R3, from above (from the fingertip side), removes the R1 loop.

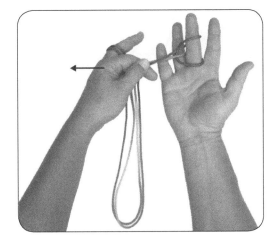

L hand moves left to tighten the cow hitch surrounding R3.

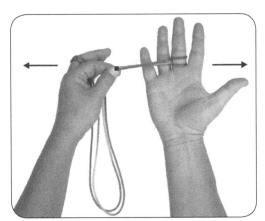

L hand releases its strings. Hands separate to reveal the cow hitches on L3 and R3.

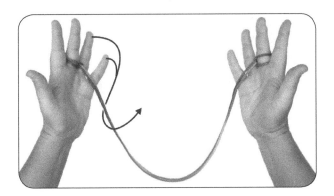

L4 and L5 pick up both L3f strings.

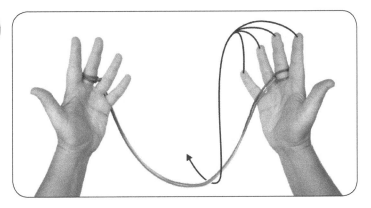

R4 and R5 bend toward you over both R3f strings. R2345, acting together, picks up both R3f strings from the near side.

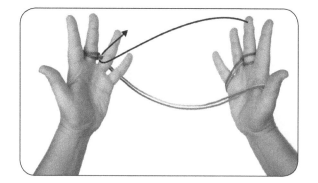

R3, passing between L3 and L4, picks up both L3f strings and returns to create a double upper R3 loop.

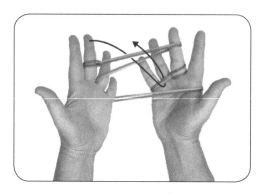

L3, through double upper R3 loop from above, picks up R45 palmar string and returns through R3 loop.

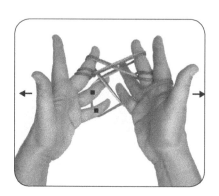

L45 releases its double loop. Hands separate slightly to absorb the slack.

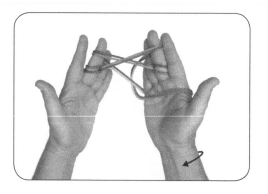

R hand rotates so that R palm faces away from you.

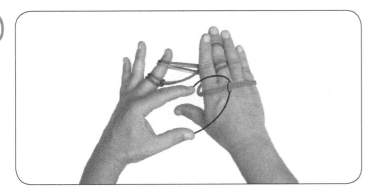

L1 and L2 grasp double R2345 dorsal string . . .

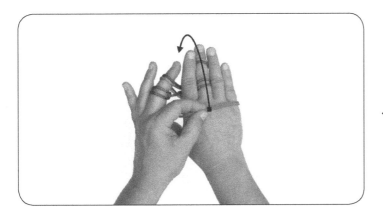

. . . remove it from the R hand . . .

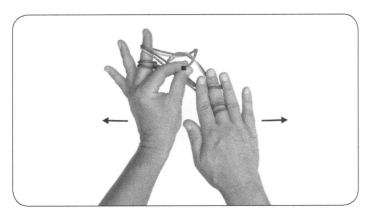

. . . and release it. Hands separate to absorb the slack.

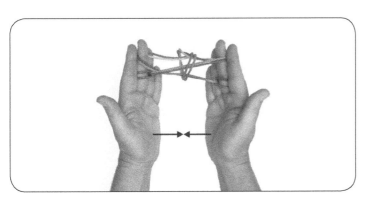

The maker chants "Small date, small date" and claps hands together.

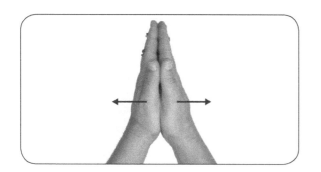

After clapping, hands separate to absorb the slack.

 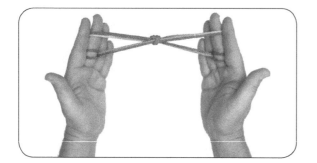

You have "Date."

 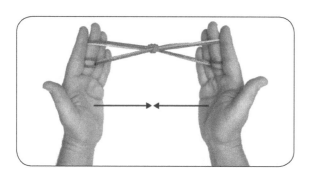

Action: Hands clap once again . . .

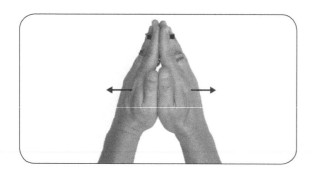

. . . then 3 releases its double upper loop just before hands separate to extend the figure.

 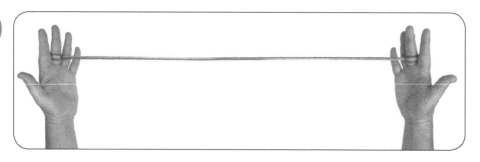

The central knot dissolves. The date has been eaten.

Lock and Key

collected by James Hornell from the people of Western India

RECOMMENDED STRING LENGTH: 1¼ SPANS

Although similar action figures are known worldwide, this action figure from India is formed by a method that is unique to Asia. The native name for this figure is *Tala Kunchi*.

When extended, the right hand of the final design represents a key and the left hand represents a dead-bolt lock. As the right hand rotates, the design near the left hand expands and contracts. The method described here has been simplified so that the maker does not have to "fish" for strings.

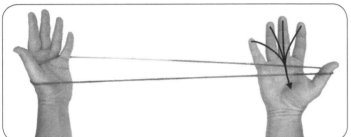

Place loop on L1, L5, and R1.

R2345 fold down to secure the R1 loop.

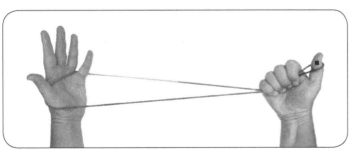

R1 releases its loop.

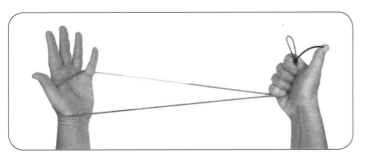

R1 presses against the base of the upright R hand loop to secure it.

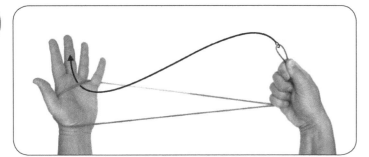

R hand passes its upright loop up and under the L palmar string.

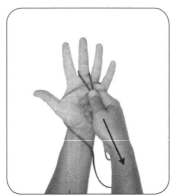

L3, from below, enters the loop held by R1 and R2.

R hand slides downward along the strings it is holding.

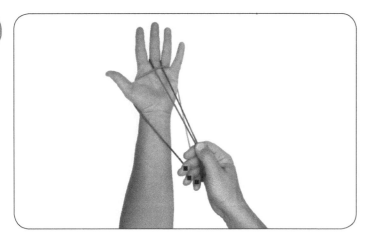

R345 withdraws from the double loop surrounding them.

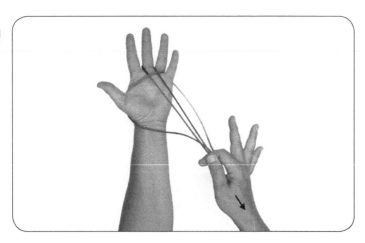

R1 and R2 slide downward along the strings they are holding to absorb the slack.

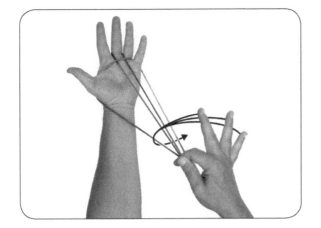

R345 hooks down all R2 strings.

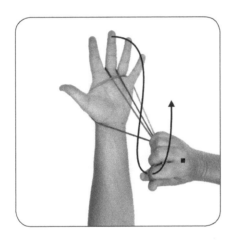

From the fingertip side, L3 removes the double R2 loop. R hand releases all strings.

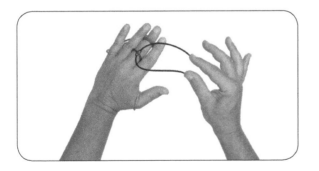

R1 and R2 grasp the lower L3 loop . . .

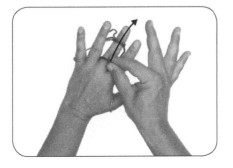

. . . lift it over the tip of L3 . . .

. . . and release it.

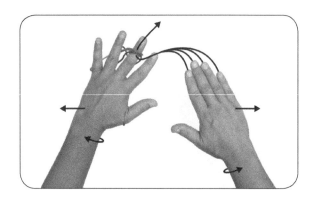

R2345, entering from below, removes the remaining double L3 loop. Hands return to the normal position (palms facing each other), but with R2345 pointing away.

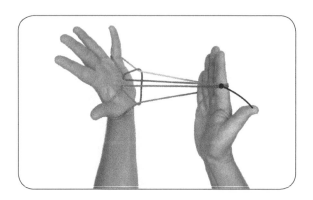

You have "Lock and Key." The L palmar string and triangles represent the deadbolt lock. The R hand represents the key.

R1 presses against double R2n strings to secure the R hand loops.

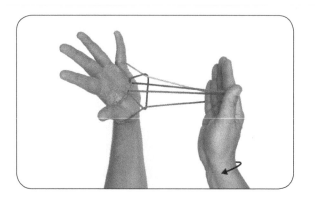

Action: R wrist rotates toward the center so that L triangles expand (deadbolt engages).

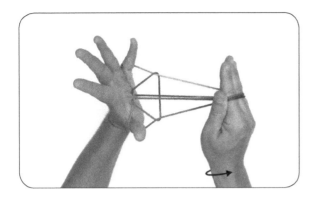

R wrist rotates away from the center so that triangles contract (dead-bolt disengages).

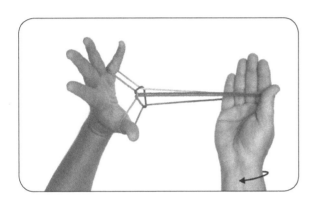

14

Continue rotating R wrist toward the center to engage . . .

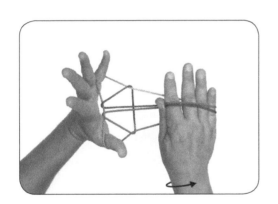

. . . and away from the center . . .

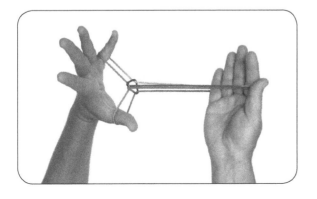

. . . to disengage the dead-bolt lock.

Scissors

collected by James Hornell from the people of Western India

RECOMMENDED STRING LENGTH: 1 SPAN

Nearly every culture has an action figure called "Scissors." In each case, two strings rub against each other like scissor blades. This example, from India, is called *katar*. It is preceded by two non-action figures: *janaja dagna* (the awning over a funeral bier) and *chasma* (a mirror).

Place loop on wrist of each hand so that near and far strings are parallel.

1, from below, picks up the far wrist string.

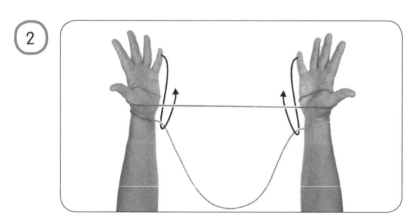

5, under 1n, picks up the near wrist string.

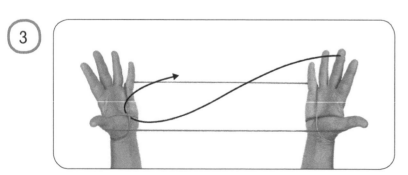

R3, from below, picks up L palmar strings where they cross.

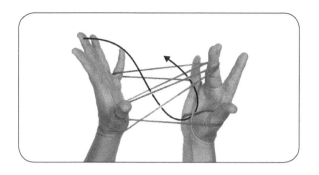

L3, through double R3 loop from above, picks up R palmar strings from below where they cross.

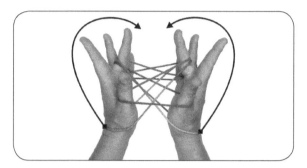

The opposite hand removes the wrist loop and releases it between the hands.

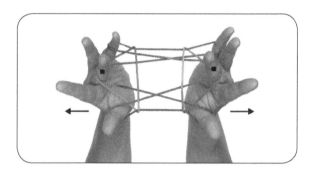

You have the "awning over a funeral bier," a three-dimensional dome-shaped figure.

To continue, release double 3 loop and extend.

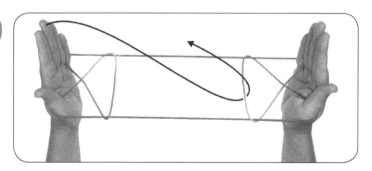

You have "mirror," a two-dimensional rectangular figure.

To continue, L3 picks up the vertical R string that spans the frame lines.

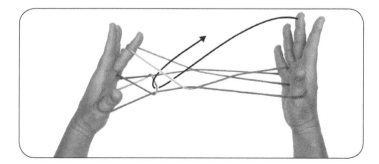

R3, through upper L3 loop from above, picks up the vertical L string that spans the frame lines.

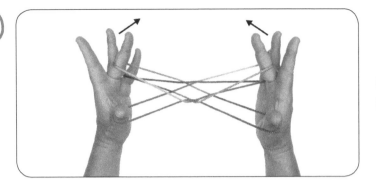

Fingers point away from you to display the final pattern.

 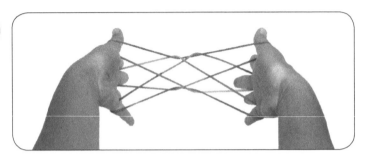

You have the Indian figure called "Scissors."

 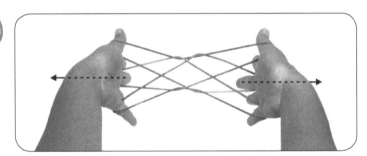

Action: To work the figure, R3 and L3 separate . . .

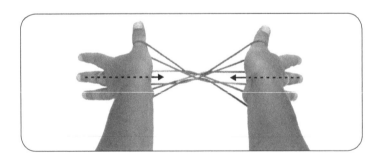

. . . so that the central diamond contracts. Then R3 and L3 approach each other . . .

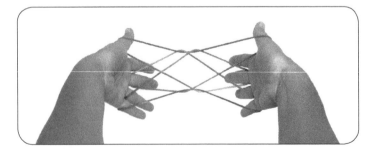

. . . so that the central diamond expands.

As the central diamond expands and contracts, it "cuts" an imaginary object much like a pair of scissors would.

Flip

collected by Will Wirt from the Navajo people of Arizona

RECOMMENDED STRING LENGTH: 1 SPAN

Among Navajo Indians, this action figure represents someone doing a flip or a somersault or jumping over a fence. Others say it represents a jumping frog. The figure is also known among the Klamath Indians of the California/Oregon border. Their method differs somewhat and is said to represent a sun that rises and sets.

①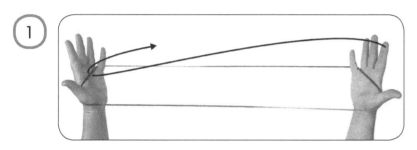
Place loop on 1 and 5 (*Position I*).

R2 picks up L palmar string.

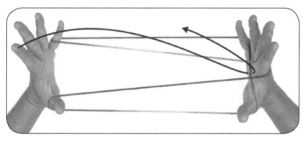
L2, through R2 loop from above, picks up R palmar string.

②
You now have *Opening A*.

2, from below, removes 1 loop.

③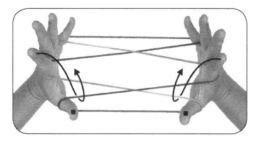
1 enters lower 2 loop from below . . .

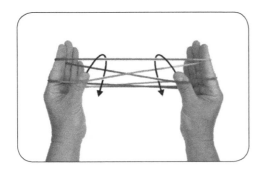

. . . and hooks down upper 2n, drawing it down through the lower 2 loop.

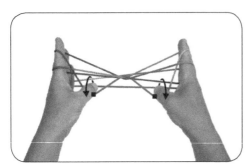

1, under intervening strings, picks up 5n and returns through hooked-down 1 loop, which slips off.

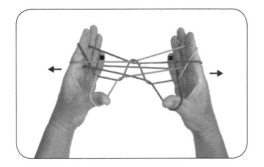

5 releases its loop. Hands separate to absorb the slack.

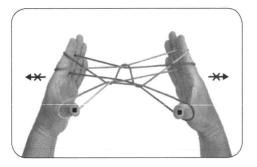

1 gently releases its loop, but hands do not separate. Released loops hang below the figure throughout the next two steps.

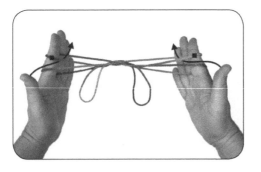

1, from below, removes the upper 2 loop.

(7)

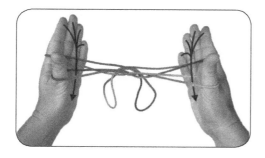

2345, passing toward you over the 2 loop, enters the 1 loop from above and hooks down 2f, 2n, and 1f.

(8)

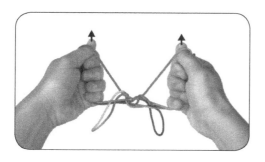

Action: With knuckles pointing away, 1 gradually applies upward pressure.

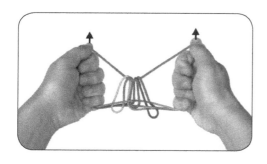

1n becomes straighter and . . .

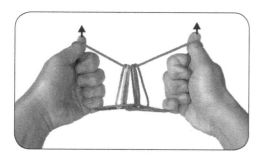

. . . straighter. Eventually the released loops flip over 1n . . .

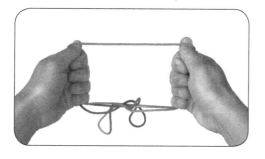

. . . and again hang below the figure.

The flip/somersault/jump is complete.

Bull Snake

collected by Will Wirt from the Navajo people of Arizona

RECOMMENDED STRING LENGTH: 1 SPAN

The bull snake is a large species of nonvenomous snake found predominantly in the Central United States. This splendid action figure from Arizona resembles a figure from the Torres Straits called "Sea-Snake." The method of construction is different, but the end result is remarkably similar.

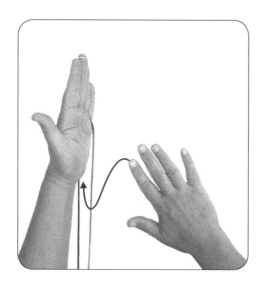

Hang the loop on L5.

R2, from below, enters the L5 loop.

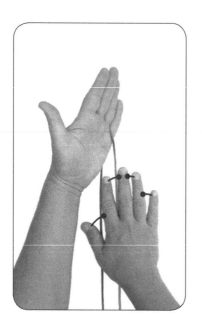

R hand fingers press against each other, trapping L5n between R2 and R3 and trapping L5f between R1 and R2.

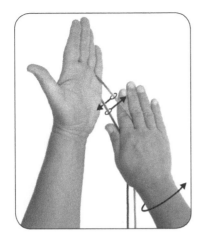

R hand rotates ¾ of a turn away from you until R2345 point toward you and L5f crosses L5n.

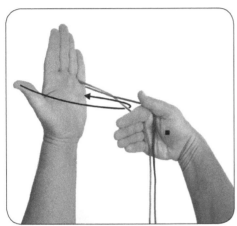

L1 picks up the segment of L5n that runs from the crossing to the R hand.

R hand releases all strings.

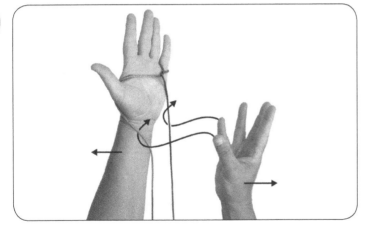

R1 and R5, from below, enter the L hanging loop and return, creating *Position I* on the R hand.

Note that the L5 loop has a full twist at its base.

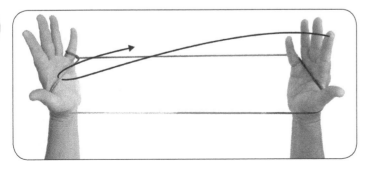

R2 picks up L palmar string.

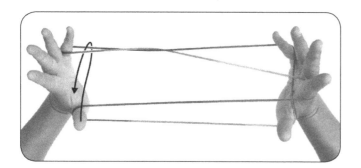

L1, under L5n, picks up L5F.

 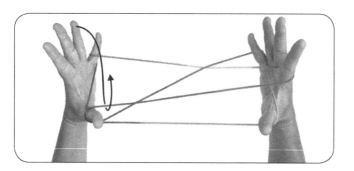

L4, over L palmar string, picks up lower L1f.

 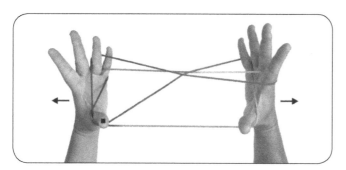

L1 releases its loops. Hands separate to absorb the slack.

 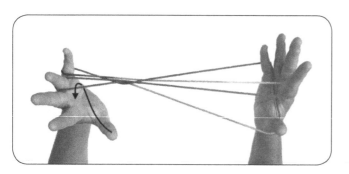

L1, from below, enters the L4 loop.

 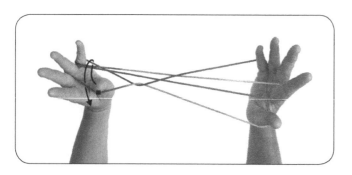

L1 passes over L4f and L5n. L1 picks up L5f and returns through the L4 loop, which slips off L1.

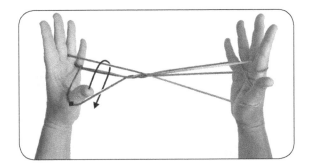

L1 hooks down L4n. The original L1 loop slips off in the process.

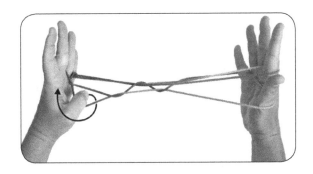

L1 catches the hooked-down string on its back by rotating toward you and up.

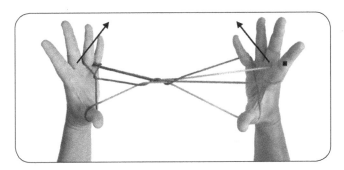

Fingers point away from you. R2 gently releases its loop.

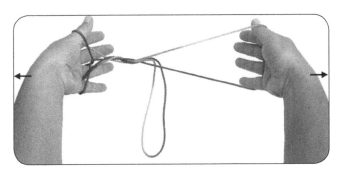

Hands separate a short distance to expand the design.

As tension is applied, the hanging loop is transformed into a "Bull Snake" that wraps around the frame lines.

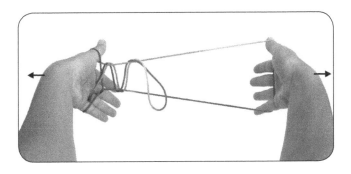

Action: Continue separating the hands, waggling the R hand as needed and allowing string to slip through the fingers of the L hand.

The "Bull Snake" begins to slither.

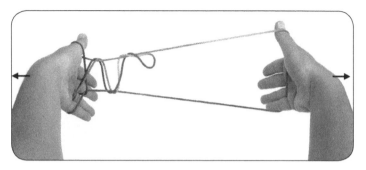

It slips around the upper and lower frame lines . . .

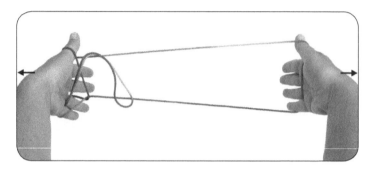

. . . as it slides toward the L hand.

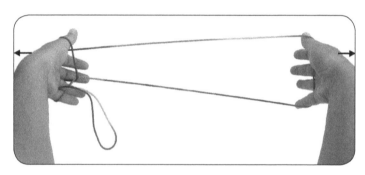

Eventually it finds a hole (the space between L4 and L5). It crawls into the hole . . .

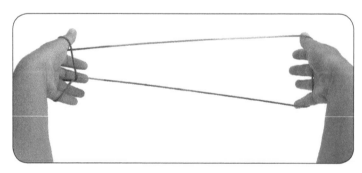

. . . and disappears.

Going to Get Some Bait

collected by Julia Averkieva from the Kwakiutl of Vancouver Island, Canada

RECOMMENDED STRING LENGTH: ¾ SPAN

The Kwakiutl Indians of Vancouver Island thrived on fish as a primary food source. In this amusing Kwakiutl action figure, a man wades into a river in search of bait. In the process, his clothes get wet and he is forced to tote them on his head.

Among the neighboring Bella Coola tribe, this figure represents a woman trying to cross a river. When she realizes how deep the water is, she hikes her skirt above her knees and proceeds to cross. Other members of the Bella Coola tribe claim that this figure represents a man with an injured leg who is teased by villagers as he tries to cross a river. In response, he magically lengthens his injured leg and crosses to spite them.

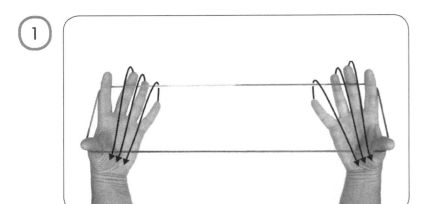

Place loop on 1 and 2.

345 hooks down 2f and 1n, closing these two strings to the palm.

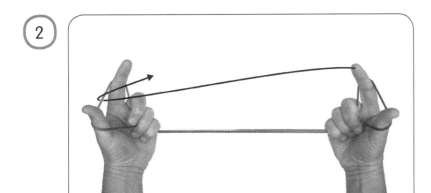

R2 picks up the short L1f–L2n string.

(3)

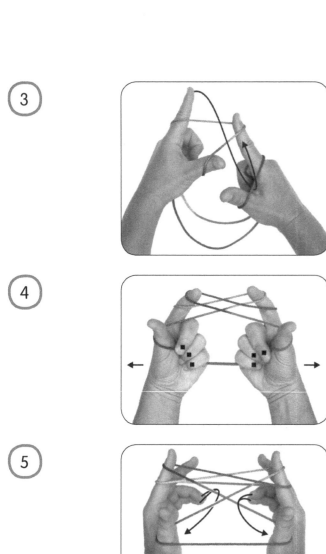

L2, over upper R2 loop, picks up the short R1f–R2n string. Make sure that this string does not slide off R2.

(4)

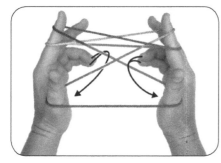

345 unfolds, releasing 1n and lower 2f. Hands separate to absorb the slack.

(5)

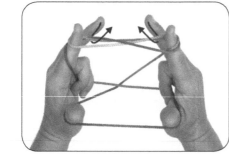

L45, under lower L2 loop, hooks down upper L2n. R45, under lower R2 loop, hooks down R1f (a continuation of upper L2n).

(6)

3, from below, enters double 2 loop.

(7)

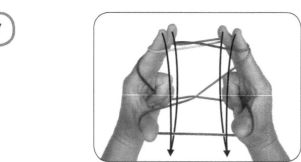

2 and 3, over intervening strings, trap 1n between their tips.

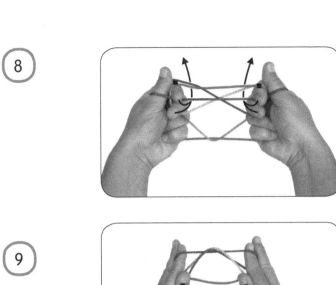

2 and 3 rotate a half turn away from you, drawing the trapped 1n string through the double 2 loop, which slips off.

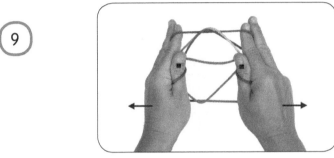

1 releases its loop. Hands separate to absorb the slack.

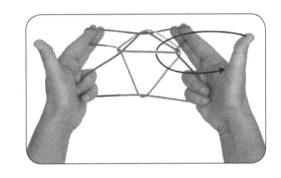

R1 hooks up the horizontal string that crosses the central diamond.

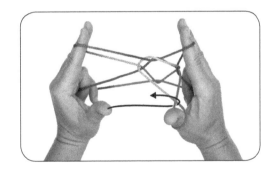

L1, from below, enters the half-twisted R1 loop and returns.

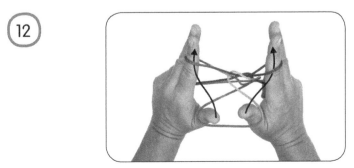

1, from below, enters the 2 loop.

Navajo 1 loops by tilting 1 toward the middle of the figure so that the lower loop slips off of 1. (If needed, use 3 to temporarily hook down all strings except lower 1n.)

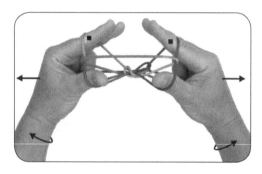

2 releases its loop. Hands separate to absorb the slack. Wrists rotate so that palms face you.

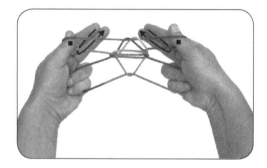

2, from below, removes 1 loop.

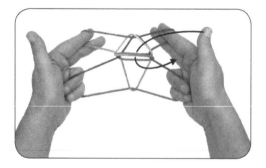

R1 hooks up the double horizontal strings that cross the near side of the central diamond.

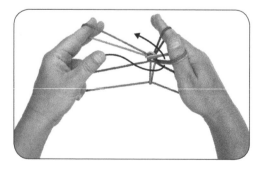

L1, from below, enters the double half-twisted R1 loop and returns.

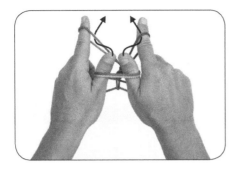

1, from below, enters the 2 loop.

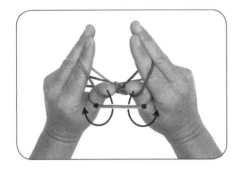

Navajo 1 loops by tilting 1 toward the middle of the figure so that the double lower loop slips off of 1. (If needed, use 3 to temporarily hook down all strings except double lower 1n.)

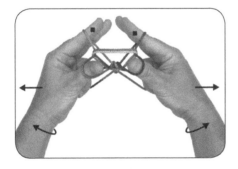

2 releases its loop. Hands separate to absorb the slack. Wrists rotate so that palms face you.

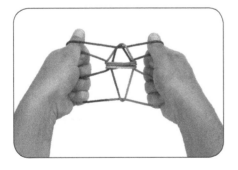

You have "Going to Get Some Bait." The central diamond represents a man cloaked in a blanket.

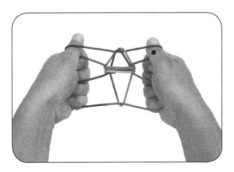

Action: R1 gently releases its loop.

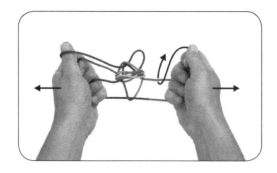

R1 picks up R45n to enlarge the R hand loop. Hands separate to absorb the slack.

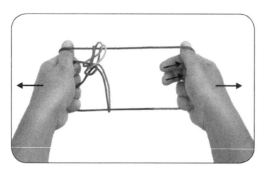

R23 joins R45 to secure the R palm string. As hands continue to separate, the man slides toward the L hand and places his wet clothes on his head.

23

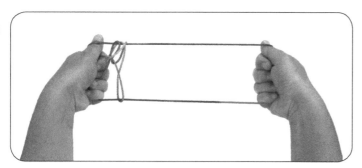

You have "Man Totes His Clothing on His Head Because It Is Wet."

Two Bear Brothers

collected by Julia Averkieva from the Kwakiutl of Vancouver Island, Canada

RECOMMENDED STRING LENGTH: ¾ SPAN

This action figure is a variation of the previous figure. In the chant that accompanies this figure, two bears, who are brothers, are hunting for moss. The little brother wants to follow the big brother, but the big brother says, "No! Don't follow me. You will only slow me down." To prove his worthiness, the little bear brother jumps past the big bear brother and becomes the leader in their quest for moss.

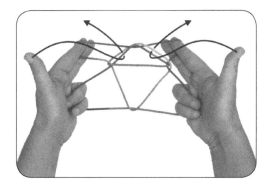

Complete steps 1–9 of "Going to Get Some Bait" (on pages 87–89).

1 picks up the upper diamond string that crosses the near side of the 2 loop.

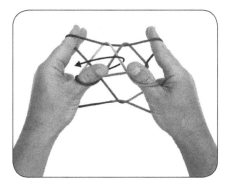

L1, from below, enters the R1 loop.

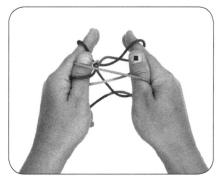

R1 releases its loop.

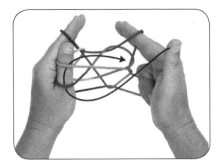

R1, from below, enters both L1 loops.

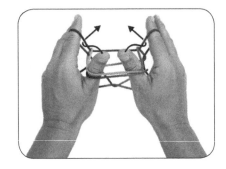

1 picks up 2n.

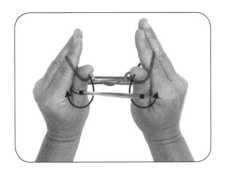

Navajo 1 loops by tilting 1 toward the middle of the figure so that the double lower loop slips off of 1. (If needed, use 3 to temporarily hook down all strings except double lower 1n.)

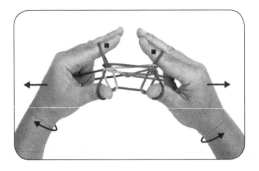

2 releases its loop. Hands separate to absorb the slack. Wrists rotate so that palms face you.

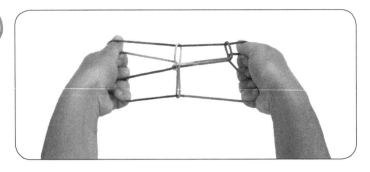

You have "Two Bear Brothers." The large vertical loop on the left represents the big brother. The small vertical loop on the right represents the little brother.

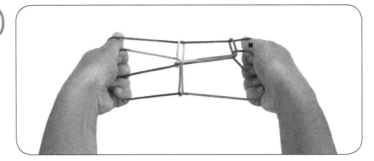

Action: R1 releases its loop.

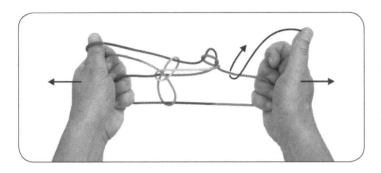

R1 picks up R45n to enlarge the R hand loop. Hands separate to absorb the slack.

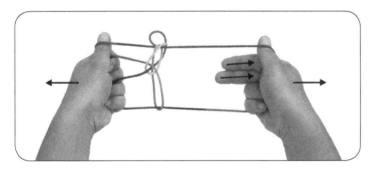

R23 joins R45 to secure the R palmar string. As hands continue to separate . . .

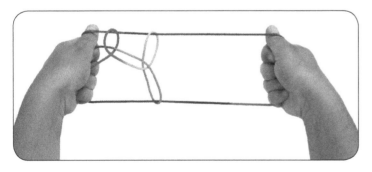

. . . the little bear brother jumps in front of the big bear brother as they travel to the left, looking for moss.

The Drying Lake

collected by Harald and Vilma Chiara Schultz from the Krahó people of Brazil

RECOMMENDED STRING LENGTH: 1 SPAN

According to ethnographer Harald Schultz and his wife, Vilma, only Krahó men make string figures. Women and girls show no interest. Whenever Vilma asked women about string figures, they told her to consult the men. They were amused that Vilma was interested in such games.

Harald Schultz filmed the Krahó on multiple occasions between 1949 and 1965. In 1964–65, he filmed four men making string figures (twenty-nine designs). The only action figure he filmed was called "The Drying Lake," which was demonstrated by Pókrók, age 28.

①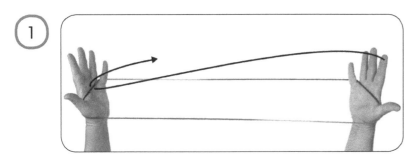

Place loop on 1 and 5 (*Position I*).

R2 picks up L palmar string.

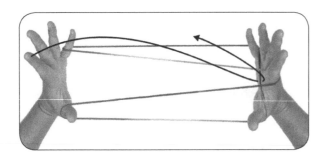

L2, through R2 loop from above, picks up R palmar string.

②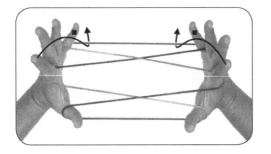

You now have *Opening A*.

2, from above, removes 5 loop.

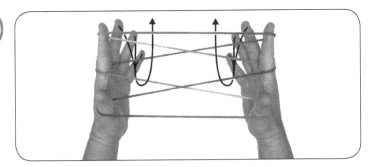

345, passing toward you under the lower 2 loop, enters the upper 2 loop from below . . .

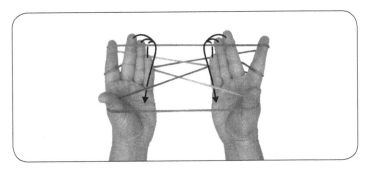

. . . and hooks down upper 2n.

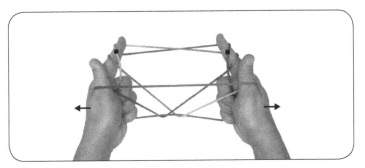

2 releases its upper loop only. Hands separate to absorb the slack.

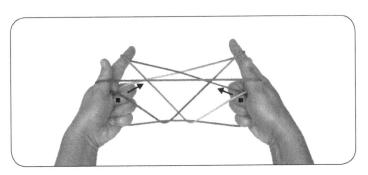

3 withdraws from the 345 loop . . .

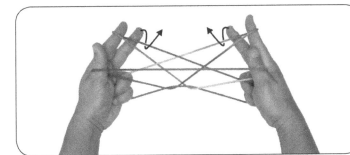

. . . and enters the 2 loop from below.

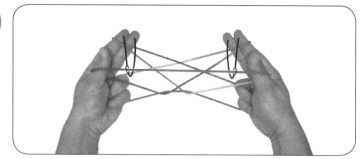

2 and 3 trap 1n between them. (3 is below the string and 2 is above it.)

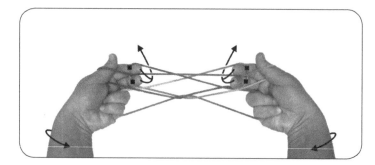

2 and 3 rotate away and up to place 1n on the back of 2. The 23 loop slips off in the process.

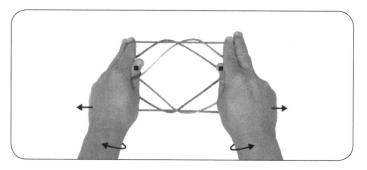

1 releases its loop. Hands separate to absorb the slack. Wrists rotate so that palms face you.

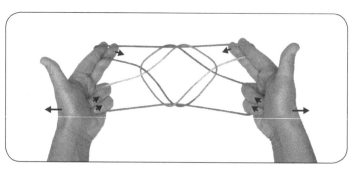

The double-walled diamond represents a lake. During a draught, the lake shrinks.

Action: To simulate water evaporating from the lake, hands momentarily loosen their grip while maintaining tension.

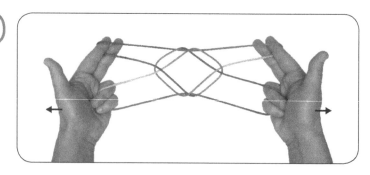

As step 8 is repeated over and over, the lake gets smaller . . .

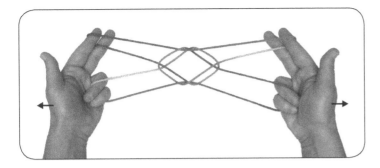

. . . and smaller . . .

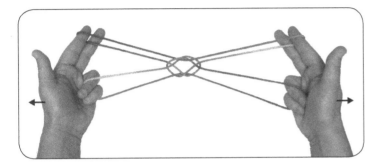

. . . and smaller . . .

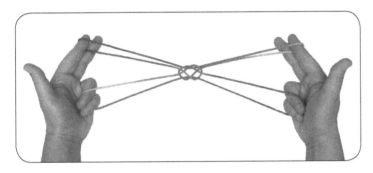

. . . until only a knot remains. The knot represents a puddle that was once a huge lake.

In Schultz's Krahó film, the "drying" action lasts nearly a minute and the motion of the performer's hands is barely detectable. This contributes to the illusion that the water in the lake is evaporating slowly.

Masked Dancers

collected by José Braunstein from the Maká people of the Gran Chaco region

RECOMMENDED STRING LENGTH: 1½ SPANS

The Maká are a group of South American Indians that once roamed the Gran Chaco—an enormous plain that occupies parts of Argentina, Bolivia, and Paraguay. Today the Maká, reduced to one-thousand two-hundred people, live in Asunción, Paraguay.

Traditionally, dance masks were made by native cultures worldwide. The mask allowed the dancer to assume the identity of an animal, spirit, or fellow human. Europeans adopted the practice, often staging elaborate "costume" or "masked" balls.

This South American action figure, which represents four masked dancers strutting from left to right, resembles a North American action figure called "Eskimos in a Dance House." However, the steps to make them are entirely different.

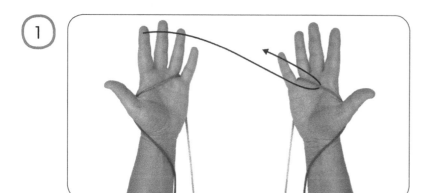

Place loop on 1 and 5 (*Position 1*).

L2 picks up R palmar string.

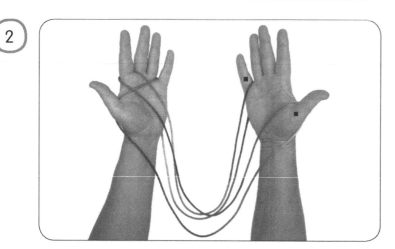

R1 and R5 release their loops, allowing them to hang below the L palm, which faces you.

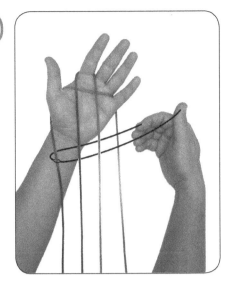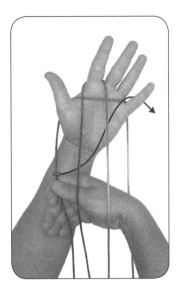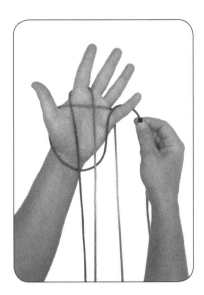

R hand, passing from right to left under L2f and L2n, grasps L1n.

R hand returns with L1n and hangs it on L5.

R hand releases the string it is holding. You now have a short "near" palmar loop formed by the string that runs from the near side of L1 to the near side of L5.

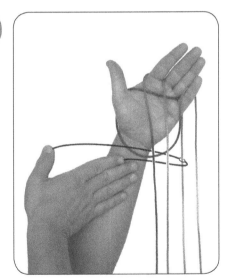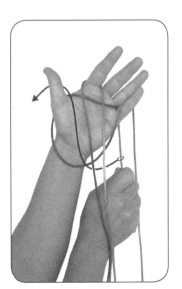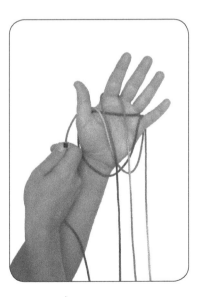

R hand, passing from left to right under L2n and L2f (and upper L5f as well), grasps lower L5f.

R hand returns with lower L5f and hangs it on L1.

R hand releases the string it is holding. You now have a short "far" palmar loop formed by the string that runs from the far side of L5 to the far side of L1.

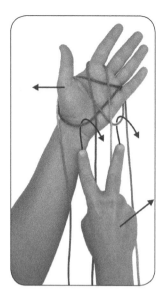

R2, passing between upper L1n and L2n, enters the near palmar loop from below.

R3, passing between L2f and upper L5f, enters the far palmar loop from below.

Hands separate to draw out the short palmar loops and fully absorb the long hanging loops.

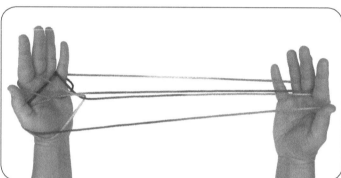

You now have single loops on L2, R2, and R3. L1 and L5 have double loops.

Release the R2 and R3 loops, then repeat steps 3–5. Since some of the strings will no longer have the same name, look at the pictures and mimic the movements.

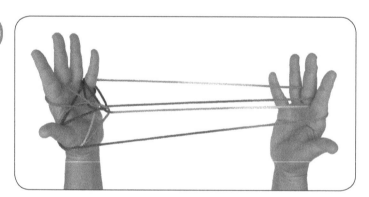

If done correctly, L1 and L5 will both acquire a third loop.

Again release the R2 and R3 loops and repeat steps 3–5.

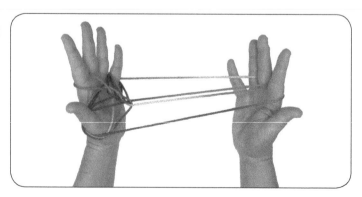

If done correctly, L1 and L5 will both acquire a fourth loop.

Again release the R2 and R3 loops and repeat steps 3–5.

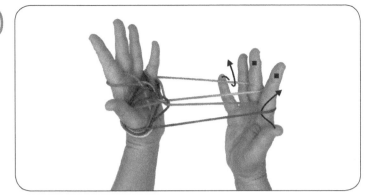

If done correctly, L1 and L5 will both acquire a fifth loop. If you started with a much longer string, keep repeating steps 3–5 until the R2 and R3 loops are short.

Now finish the figure:

R1, from below, removes the R2 loop. R5, from below, removes the R3 loop.

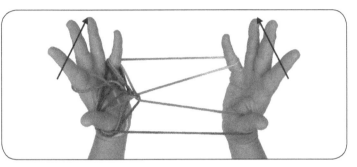

Fingers point away from you to obtain a better view of the L1 loops.

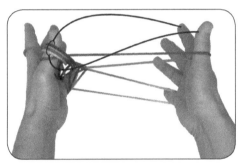

R1 and R2 grasp all the loops that were added to L1 in steps 3–8. These are easily identified because none of them has a string that runs directly to R1.

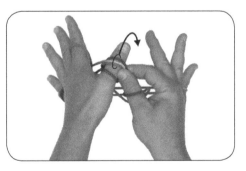

R hand removes the added loops from L1 . . .

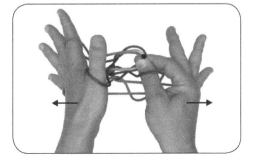

. . . and releases them.

Hands separate to absorb the slack.

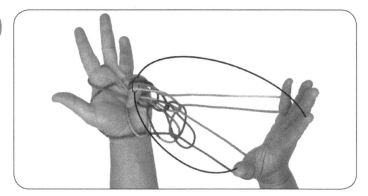

Likewise R1 and R2 grasp all the loops that were added to L5 in steps 3–8. (You may need to point L5 toward you to obtain a better view of its loops.) The added loops are easily identified because none of them has a string that runs directly to R5.

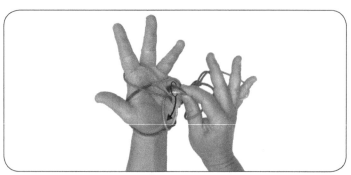

R hand removes the added loops from L5 . . .

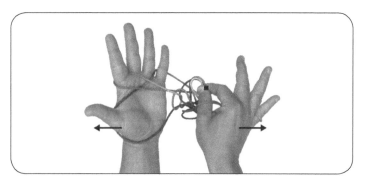

. . . and releases them. Hands separate to absorb the slack.

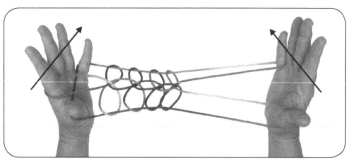

To display the figure, fingers point away from you . . .

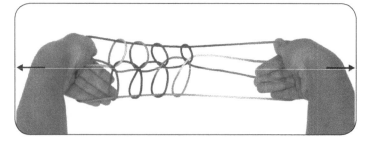

. . . while hands separate to sharpen the design.

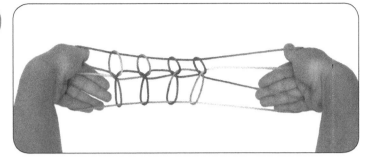

According to the Maká, the linked loops represent four "Masked Dancers" waiting to perform.

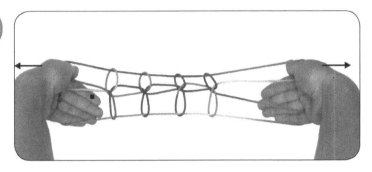

Action: Release the L2 loop and gently separate the hands.

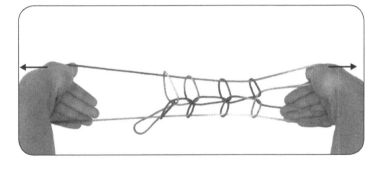

The dancers will strut from left to right . . .

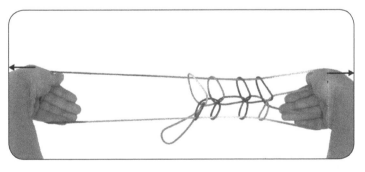

. . . while onlookers sing and admire their beautiful masks and costumes.

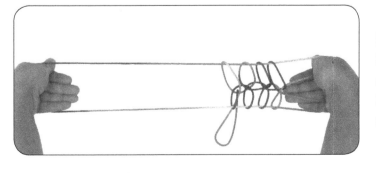

Don't be afraid to adapt this figure to better suit your audience. You could claim that it represents four ballerinas holding hands as they tiptoe across a stage (as in *Swan Lake*).

A Crab

collected by Walter E. Roth from the Warrau people of Guyana

RECOMMENDED STRING LENGTH: 1 SPAN

Crabs are greedy and quarrelsome. They often walk sideways and love to hide in holes and crevices to avoid being eaten. Those features are humorously captured in this string figure from Guyana. Like many South American string figures, the design is formed somewhat mechanically, with one hand manipulating the loops and strings of another. The figure lacks right-left symmetry, but the resulting upper-lower symmetry is ideal for creating design motifs that slide.

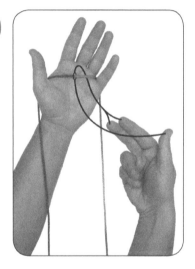 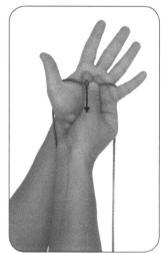

Place loop on L1 and L5 (*Position I* on the left hand only).

With R palm facing you, R1 and R23 grasp the L palmar string . . .

. . . and draw it out slightly.

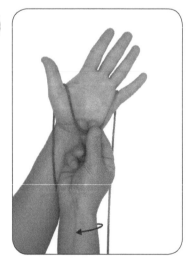 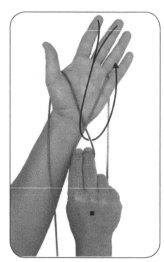

You now have a short palmar loop. R hand rotates to introduce a half twist into the short loop so that L5n crosses over L1f.

R hand releases the half-twisted loop onto L23.

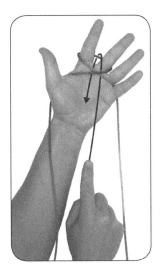

R2, passing under the crossed palmar strings and between the fork of L2 and L3, hooks down the L23 dorsal string and draws it out slightly.

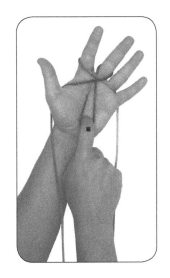 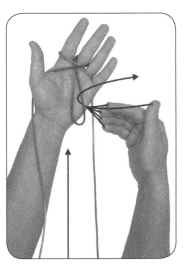

R2 releases its loop.

R hand enters the released loop from below and moves to the right to fully absorb the long hanging loop.

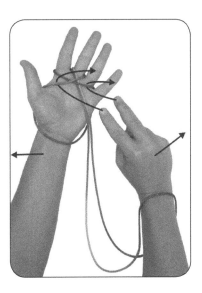

The long hanging loop is now a short string that crosses the L wrist.

R2 picks up L1f while R3 picks up L5n. Hands separate to draw out these two strings.

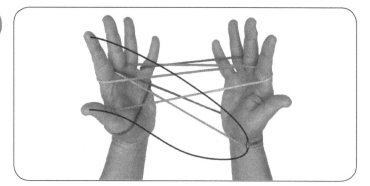

L1 and L2 grasp R wrist loop . . .

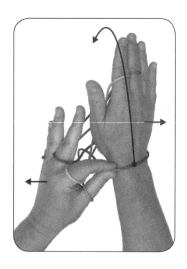

. . . and remove it from the R hand. Hands separate to absorb the released loop.

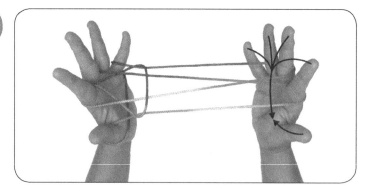

R hand fingers form a fist, pressing all R2 and R3 strings against the palm.

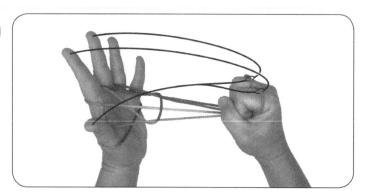

L1 and L23 grasp the strings on the backs on R2 and R3 . . .

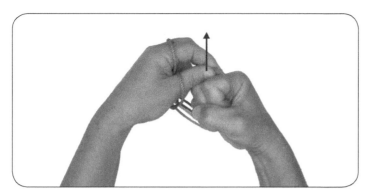

. . . and raise them to form short upright loops.

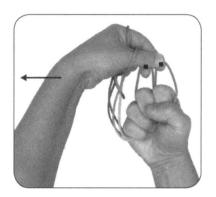

L1 and L23 release the strings they are holding. L hand returns to the left.

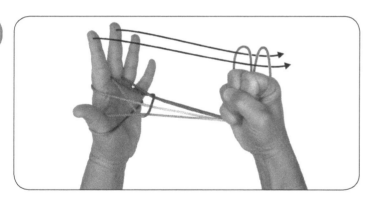

L2, from above (from the fingertip side), enters the R2 loop. L3, also from above, enters the R3 loop.

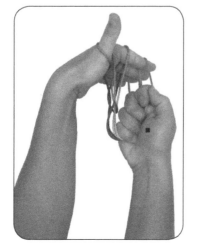

R hand releases all strings, creating upper L2 and upper L3 loops.

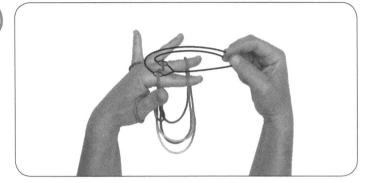

R1 and R23 grasp the lower strings on the backs on L2 and L3.

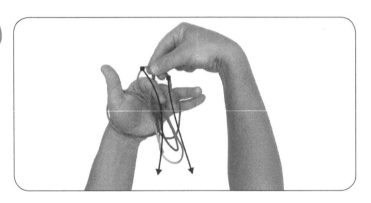

R hand lifts the lower L2 and L3 loops over the upper L2 and L3 loops . . .

. . . and releases them (i.e., Navajo the loops).

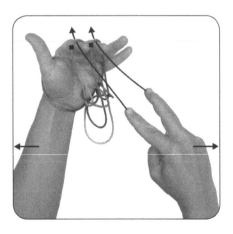

R2, from above (from the fingertip side), removes the L2 loop. R3, also from above, removes the L3 loop. Hands gently separate to absorb the slack.

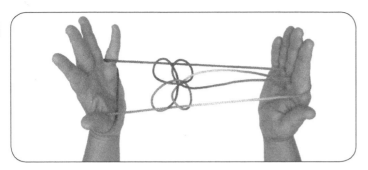

When extended gently, a clover-shaped figure that represents the Warrau "Crab" appears between the hands.

Hint: Keep R2 pressed against R3 to prevent the crab from moving.

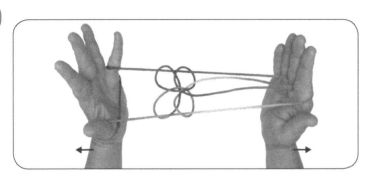

Action: To make the crab crawl, continue separating the hands, allowing strings to slip around R2 and R3.

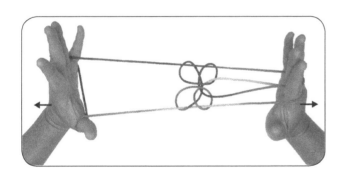

The crab will scuttle from left to right . . .

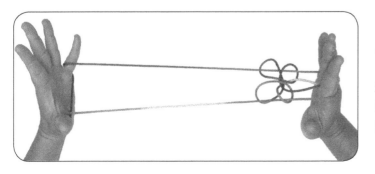

. . . looking for a place to hide.

Suggestion: At the end of the story, fold R23 down over the crab to provide a hiding place.

A Little Bird

collected by R. Martínez-Crovetto from the Araucanos of Patagonia, Argentina

RECOMMENDED STRING LENGTH: 1½ SPANS

In his article on string figures from Patagonia, Dr. Martínez-Crovetto describes three closely related action figures that represent birds in flight. In each case, ring fingers are flexed up and down to fold and unfold the figure in half along a horizontal axis that represents the bird's spine. The author was unable to identify the exact bird that this figure represents; his informant used the word *chiwil*.

String figures that begin with two loops on the index fingers are known worldwide. In the literature on Pacific Island figures, this opening is often called the *Murray Opening*. After forming, the opening fingers of each hand act in unison, but they often pick up different strings. The instructions seem complicated, but the figure is quite simple.

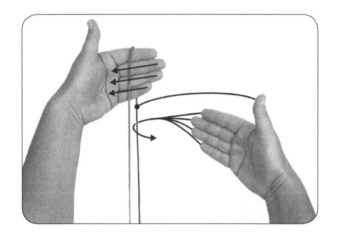

With L palm facing you and fingers pointing right, hang the loop on L2345.

R hand grasps L2345f. R1 presses against R2 to secure the held string.

L345 secures L2345n by clutching this string against the L palm.

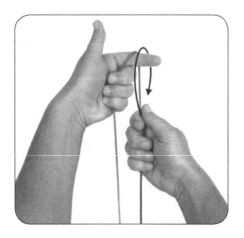

R hand wraps the string it is holding a full turn clockwise around L2, forming a tight loop that surrounds the tip of L2.

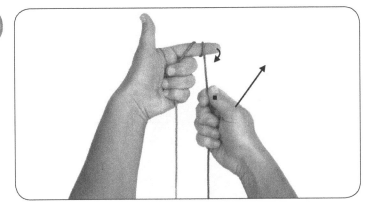

L2 bends so that its tip points toward you. R hand moves up and to the right so that hands are level. R1 releases its grip and points upward.

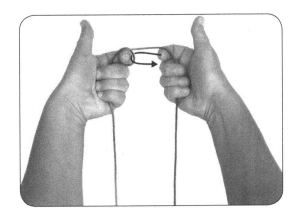

While remaining within its loop, R2, from below (from the knuckle side), enters the tight loop surrounding the tip of L2.

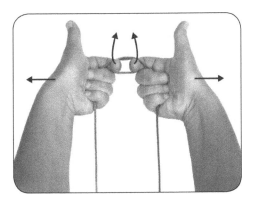

2 of each hand rotates up. 345 loosens its grip so that the string can flow into the double 2 loop as hands begin to separate.

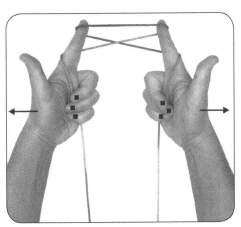

345 releases its grip entirely as hands separate to absorb the hanging loop.

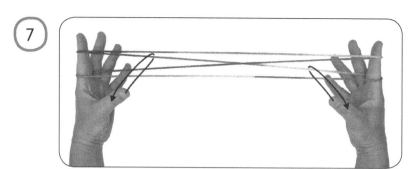

You have the *Murray Opening*, named after a small island in the Torres Straits where it was first recorded.

L1 and R1 pass between the upper and lower 2n strings. L1 picks up upper L2f, while R1 picks up lower R2f.

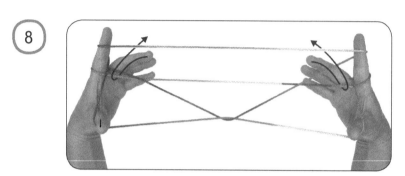

L3, passing over lower L2f, picks up lower L2n while R3, passing over upper R2f, picks up lower R2n.

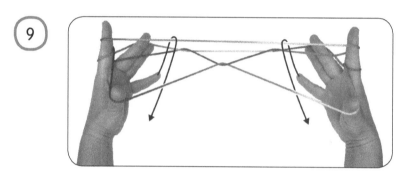

L5, passing under lower L2f and L3f, hooks down upper L2n. R5, passing under upper R2f and R3f, hooks down upper R2n.

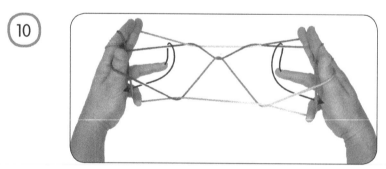

L4, passing under L3f, hooks down lower L2f. R4, passing under R3f, hooks down upper R2f. On each hand, 4 passes behind the 5n string before touching the palm.

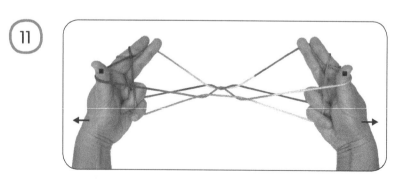

1 releases its loop. Hands separate to absorb the slack.

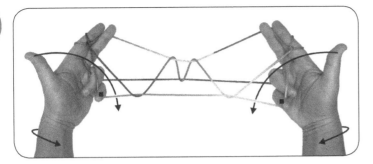

1, passing under all intervening strings, removes the 5 loop from the fingertip side.

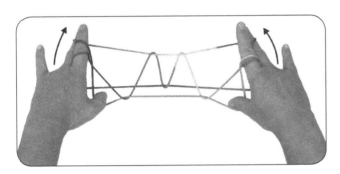

You have a three-dimensional pattern that represents "A Little Bird." Its head is on the right and its tail is on the left.

Action: To simulate the flapping of the little bird's wings, 4 points up . . .

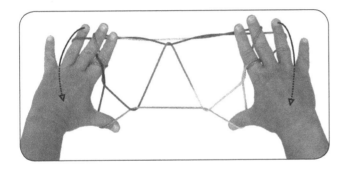

. . . then down. The dotted segment of the arrow indicates that the path of 4 is on the far side of the palm.

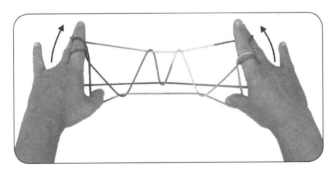

At first, flexing your ring finger may prove difficult . . .

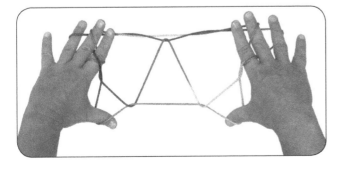

. . . but the charm of this simple figure will motivate you to acquire new dexterity!

A Spider

collected by José Braunstein from the Maká people of the Gran Chaco region

Recommended String Length: 1½ spans

This amusing action figure, which represents a big spider crawling up your arm, is unlike any other in the literature. Its overall form is quite simple: a coil of string that slides up and down vertical frame lines. Describing how to make it using standard string figure terminology is tedious since so many minor manipulations are required. Perhaps knot-tying terminology would work better!

Once you learn how to make this figure, you can invent your own method if you forget the one described here. It's unlikely that the method described here is followed exactly by all Gran Chaco string figure makers. Because the design motif of this string figure is so elemental (a simple circle that slides), it is easily adapted. It could represent a rising sun or moon or a helium-filled balloon that a child accidentally releases. If displayed upside-down, it could represent the illuminated ball in Times Square that signals the beginning of a new year.

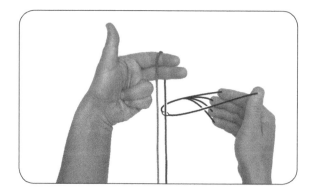

With L palm facing you and L45 pressed against the palm, hang the loop on L23, which points right.

R hand grasps L23f. R1 presses against R2 to secure the held string.

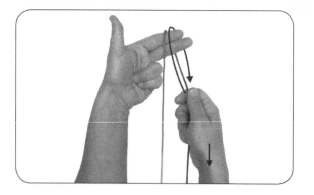

R hand wraps the held string a full turn around L23, sliding down along the string as it completes the wrap.

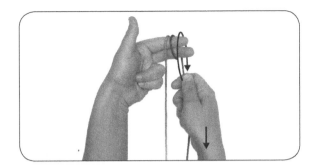

Again R hand wraps the held string a full turn around L23, sliding down along the string as it completes the wrap.

 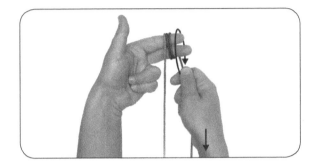

R hand wraps the held string around the tip of L23 six more times.

 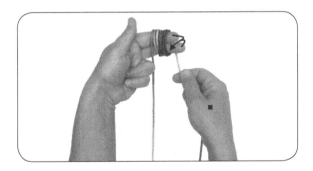

L23 points toward you as R hand releases the string it is holding.

R1 and R2 grasp the far strings of the coil surrounding L23.

 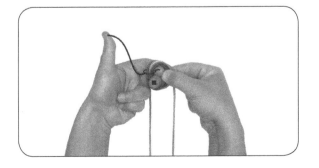

Similarly, L1 and L2 grasp the near strings of the coil. L3 withdraws from the coil.

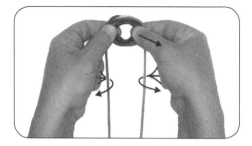

R12 slides down along the right string of the hanging loop while R345 closes this string to the palm. L345 closes the left string of the hanging loop to the L palm.

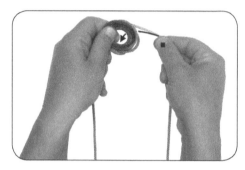

R1 releases its grip on the held string. From the far side, R2 pushes it through the coil held by L1 and L2.

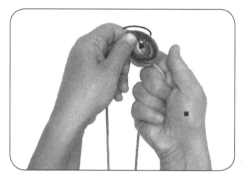

R hand releases all strings. L2 replaces R2 as the "pushing" finger.

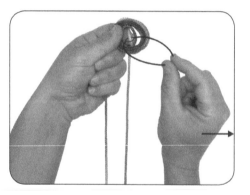

From the near side, R1 and R2 grasp the pushed string and draw it slightly to the right.

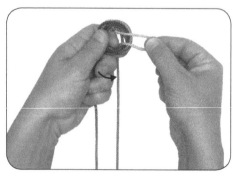

L3, releasing its grip, unfolds so that it can push the right string of the hanging loop.

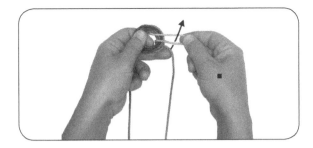

From the far side, L3 pushes the right string of the hanging loop through the loop held by R12 to create an L3 loop. R hand releases its grip.

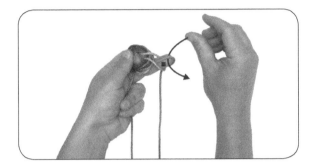

From the far side, R1 removes the L3 loop.

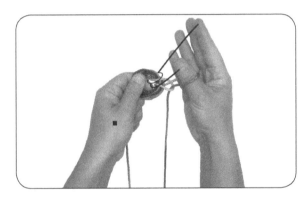

R1 and R2 grasp the coil held by L1 and L2. L hand releases its grip.

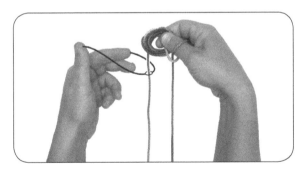

L1 and L2 grasp the left string of the hanging loop.

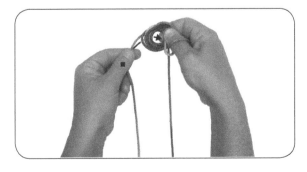

L1 releases its grip on the held string. From the far side, L2 pushes it through the coil held by the R hand.

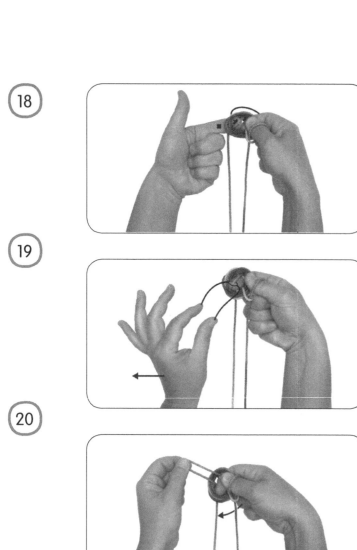

(18) R2 replaces L2 as the "pushing" finger.

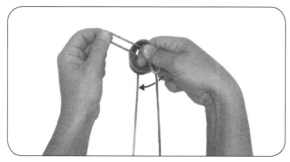

(19) From the near side, L1 and L2 grasp the pushed string and draw it to the left.

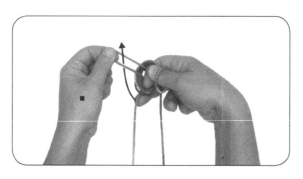

(20) R3 unfolds so that it can push the left string of the hanging loop.

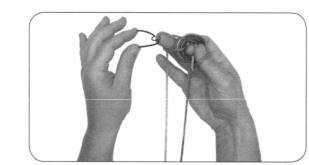

(21) From the far side, R3 pushes the left string of the hanging loop through the loop held by L12 to create an R3 loop. L hand releases its grip.

(22) L1 and L2 grasp the R3 loop.

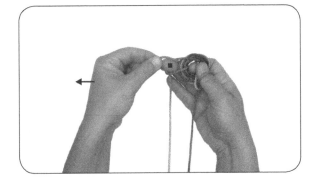

R3 releases its "pushed" loop as L1 and L2 draw it to the left.

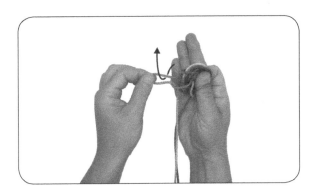

From the far side, R5 enters the loop held by L12.

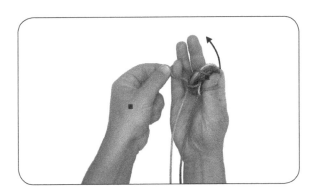

L12 releases the loop it is holding onto R5. At the same time, R12 releases its grip on the coil.

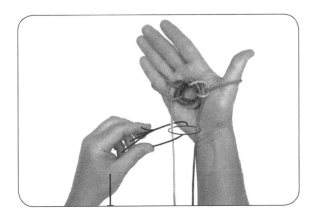

L hand grasps both strings of the hanging loop and pulls them down to tighten the coil.

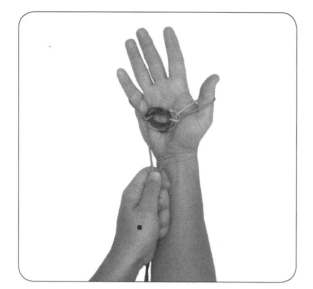

L hand releases its grip.

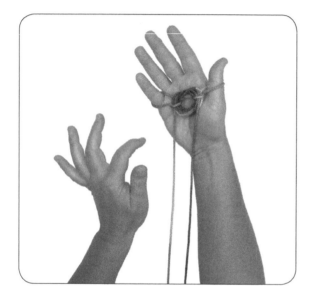

The coil on the right palm represents a big, hairy, scary "Spider"!

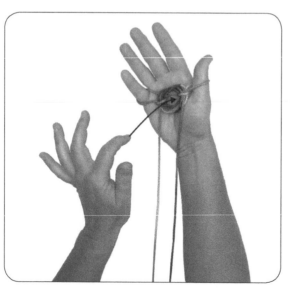

Action Setup: From the near side, L2 enters the coil.

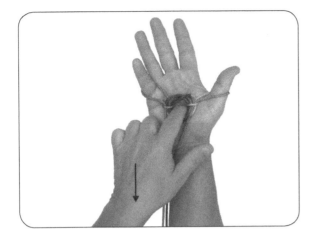

L2 drags the coil down along the two strings of the hanging loop . . .

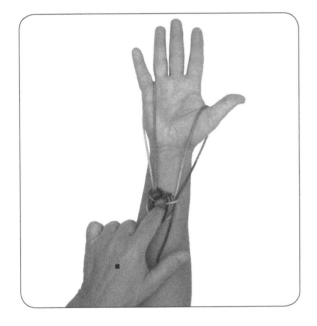

. . . and releases it.

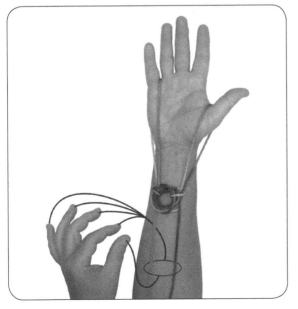

Action: To make the spider climb up your R arm, L hand grasps both strings of the hanging loop . . .

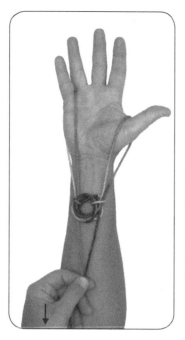
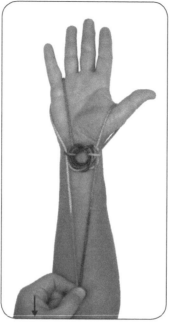

. . . and pulls them down. The coil will slide upward, eventually returning to the right palm.

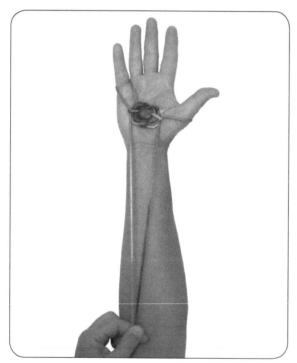

Repeat steps 27–31 as often as desired to make the spider crawl up your right arm.

To "catch" the spider, form a fist when the coil reaches your palm.

Storytellers can use this string figure to illustrate the "Itsy Bitsy Spider." In the nursery rhyme, the spider climbs up the spout of a rain gutter.